"Authentic, real, honest, raw, hopeful, and helpful; *Love Is!* faces the difficult and dark side of grief with courage and relational integrity."
—Karen Nicola
Grief educator/coach

"This book is a gift to the world. *Love Is!* is the story of grief drenched in celebration—a masterpiece of emotional self-analysis."
—Ty Gibson
President, Light Bearers

"*Love Is!* rises above most biblically oriented books about death and allows space and freedom for the negative emotions that must be felt when such a profound loss is experienced. *Love Is!* provides a front row seat to the inevitable pain such loss delivers, but through transparency and intense vulnerability, leaves the reader feeling seen, comforted, and filled with hope."
—Sarah C. Otis
Licensed clinical psychologist

"By sharing with us the deep emotional, social, and religious struggles he experienced in losing his beloved wife, Frank Hasel offers us priceless wisdom, practical advice, and religious insights that will assist those going through a similar devastating experience to find constructive ways to cope with their grief. The book is indispensable reading for clergy, counselors, and any person involved in clinical work for the terminally ill."
—Ángel Manuel Rodriguez
Former director, Biblical Research Institute

"As a medical practitioner and pastor, I welcome this well-written and user-friendly resource for healthcare providers, pastors, chaplains, and for those experiencing loss. The ideas shared are practical, realistic, doable, and based on firsthand experience. Implementing the 'helpful help' suggestions can aid those not trained as grief counselors to apply them in their own lives and can guide them in their interaction with those bereaved. The book will be a great blessing across a wide audience. I highly recommend it."

—Peter N. Landless
Director, General Conference Adventist Health Ministries

"Frank Hasel's *Love Is!* is essential reading for chaplains, pastors, and practitioners as well as those who aspire to express compassion, care, and love to those grieving the loss of their soulmate. *Love Is!* provides genuine practical insights into how to minister effectively and sensitively to the real needs of the grieving. It is accessible yet profound."

—Anthony R. Kent
Associate ministerial secretary, General Conference of Seventh-day Adventists

"While sorrow and loss are common to the human experience, rarely is someone able to allow others into their experience as powerfully as Frank Hasel. Frank has given us an emotional word picture that is powerfully vivid in color, shape, and texture, a picture that evokes a personal response of worship and adoration to our Lord Jesus Christ, a man of sorrows, one who was acquainted with grief."

—L. Ann Hamel
Psychologist

LOVE IS!

LOVE IS!

A Journey of Grief, Grace, and Gratitude

FRANK M. HASEL

Foreword by
NICHOLAS WOLTERSTORFF

CASCADE *Books* • Eugene, Oregon

LOVE IS!
A Journey of Grief, Grace, and Gratitude

Copyright © 2024 Frank M. Hasel. All rights reserved. Except for brief quotations in critical publications or reviews, no part of this book may be reproduced in any manner without prior written permission from the publisher. Write: Permissions, Wipf and Stock Publishers, 199 W. 8th Ave., Suite 3, Eugene, OR 97401.

Cascade Books
An Imprint of Wipf and Stock Publishers
199 W. 8th Ave., Suite 3
Eugene, OR 97401

www.wipfandstock.com

PAPERBACK ISBN: 978-1-6667-8237-0
HARDCOVER ISBN: 978-1-6667-8238-7
EBOOK ISBN: 978-1-6667-8239-4

Cataloguing-in-Publication data:

Names: Hasel, Frank M. | Wolterstorff, Nicholas.

Title: Love is! : A journey of grief, grace, and gratitude. / Frank M. Hasel.

Description: Eugene, OR: Cascade Books, 2024 | Includes bibliographical references.

Identifiers: ISBN 978-1-6667-8237-0 (paperback) | ISBN 978-1-6667-8238-7 (hardcover) | ISBN 978-1-6667-8239-4 (ebook)

Subjects: LCSH: Bereavement—Religious aspects—Christianity. |Grief. | Loss (Psychology). |

Classification: BV4905.2 .H375 2024 (paperback) | BV4905.2 (ebook)

VERSION NUMBER 041124

For my three sons

Jonathan,

Florian,

and

Daniel,

who have been

brave fellow travelers on the journey of grief and loss

Contents

Permissions | ix
Foreword by Nicholas Wolterstorff | xi
Preface | xiii
Acknowledgments | xv

Falling | xvii

Chapter 1: Dealing With the Unspeakable | 1

Chapter 2: Tragic Events Often Start Unexpectedly | 7

Chapter 3: Diagnosis | 9

Chapter 4: Facing the Unknown | 19

Chapter 5: Hope Frustrated | 25

Chapter 6: Facets and Feelings of Loss and Grief | 33

Chapter 7: Learning to Talk about Death and Grief | 43

Chapter 8: Death's Impact: A World Turned Inside Out | 55

Chapter 9: Myths of Closure | 67

Chapter 10: Learning Lessons | 71

Chapter 11: Lovingly Moving Forward | 85

Chapter 12: Don't Say It! | 89

Chapter 13: Helpful Help! | 99

Chapter 14: Time Is a Wound | 103

Chapter 15: Epilogue | 113

Bibliography | 115

Permissions

Scripture quotations marked ESV from The ESV® Bible (The Holy Bible, English Standard Version®), copyright © 2001 by Crossway, a publishing ministry of Good News Publishers. Used by permission. All rights reserved.

Scripture quotations marked GNT are from the Good News Translation in Today's English Version, Second Edition Copyright © 1992 by American Bible Society. Used by Permission.

Scripture quotations marked NASB are from New American Standard Bible®, Copyright © 1960, 1971, 1977, 1995, 2020 by The Lockman Foundation. Used by permission. All rights reserved.

Scripture quotations marked NIV are from the New International Version®. Copyright© 1984, by Biblica, Inc.™. Used by permission of Zondervan.

Scripture quotations marked NKJV are from the New King James Version®. Copyright © 1982 by Thomas Nelson. Used by permission. All rights reserved.

Scripture quotations marked NLT are from the Holy Bible, New Living Translation, copyright ©1996, 2004, 2015 by Tyndale House Foundation. Used by permission of Tyndale House Publishers, Carol Stream, Illinois 60188. All rights reserved.

Scripture quotations marked The Message are from *THE MESSAGE*. Copyright© 1993, 1994, 1995, 1996, 2000, 2001, 2002. Used by permission of NavPress Publishing Group.

Foreword

FRANK HASEL'S *LOVE IS! A Journey of Grief, Grace, and Gratitude* is the story of the death of the author's wife by cancer more than a decade ago, and of the grief over that loss that he has lived with during the subsequent years. After noting that "much of what we learn in life comes to us in the form of stories," he writes: "My story has become a melody in my own heart that I can share with my children—and the children of my children—and with you," the reader.[1]

The story Hasel tells is utterly honest. He observes that many Christians "find it difficult to express their true feelings when facing tragedy, suffering, and loss. Instead, many say what they think Christians ought to say in the face of adversity."[2] Not so this author. In the course of reading the book we come to know his innermost thoughts and feelings. Christians, he writes, "need to discover the grace and blessing of the biblical art of lament in dealing with suffering, injustice, and the pain of death."[3] Hasel's story is a sustained lament.

There are available on the market today a fair number of open and candid stories by Christians of the loss and grief they have experienced. *Love Is!* stands out from the crowd.

It is distinctive in the acuity of its perception of the multiple dimensions of grief, and in the extraordinary felicity of its descriptions of those dimensions. We come away with an expanded awareness of the complexity of grief, and of how each person's grief, while resembling that of others, is nonetheless unique.

---

1. Hasel, *Love Is!*, 2.
2. Hasel, *Love Is!*, 46.
3. Hasel, *Love Is!*, 46.

Love Is!

It is also distinctive in that, every now and then, the author suspends the telling of the story to reflect in depth on some dimension of his thoughts and feelings. These set pieces are little gems. When he and his wife are dealing with the diagnosis and treatment of her cancer, they experience a great deal of waiting; that leads Hasel to a wonderful meditation on waiting. He notices that in his grief he is envious of those who are not grieving; that leads to a meditation on envy. He finds that he is much more fearful than formerly; that leads to a meditation on fear. He finds that he is now called, and treated as, a "widower"; that leads him to reflect on how difficult he finds it to live into this new identity. He finds his grief suffused with longing for a new day; that leads to a meditation on the place of such longing in life. He finds himself slowly learning again to be grateful; that leads to a sustained meditation on the importance of gratitude. He discovers that there is a mysterious balming effect in writing about his grief; that leads to a meditation on the power of writing for the person doing the writing. Little gems, these and other set pieces of meditation and reflection.

And the book is distinctive in that, toward the end, the author interrupts the story to offer advice on how to help the person in grief: what to say and what not to say, what to do and what not to do. He gives examples from his own experience of what he calls *helpful help* and examples of what was not helpful help.

It is, indeed, a story—honest, gripping. But it's more than a story, much more.

Nicholas Wolterstorff
Noah Porter Professor of Philosophical Theology emeritus,
Yale University
Senior research fellow, Institute for Advanced Studies in Culture,
University of Virginia

Preface

THE EXPERIENCE OF LOSS is something that we all encounter in one way or another. No life runs entirely smoothly. Not everything in life is fair. We all face losses on various levels. We may lose our job and with it our regular income and financial security. We may face the loss of relationships or close friends and with it our sense of belonging and safety. We may lose our belongings in a raging fire or the devastating effects of natural disasters. We may struggle with the loss of our health, or we may be traumatized by an accident leaving us handicapped. We may lose our good reputation or a significant contest that is important to us. The list of losses in life is endless. Unfortunately, some losses have more lasting impacts than others.

Early in the process of writing this book, I decided to block several hours every week for this project. Those precious moments were extraordinarily productive, and I made good progress. I distinctly remember how satisfied I was with how the ideas flowed, and I felt I found the right words to describe my feelings and experience. I regularly saved what I wrote, and I had a triple backup, just to be on the safe side. Suddenly, for some inexplicable reason, my computer froze. When I rebooted and attempted to continue where I had left off, I realized that several pages and more than 7,500 words were lost. I checked the backups, but they were gone. I turned to the IT specialists for help, but the file was lost. This irrecoverable loss of unique words and several days of hard work was a severe setback for my writing and left me wondering if I would be able to come up with similarly persuasive expressions to describe what loss through death has done to me.

As frustrating as this loss was for me, it is unspeakably insignificant and trivial in comparison to losing the person I loved most, my wife. It simply illustrates the fact that we are all confronted with different losses throughout our lives. The fact that you are reading this book indicates that you relate to loss in your life in one way or another. Indeed, facing loss on different levels creates a fellowship in this experience and connects us to our common humanity. Even if you have not experienced the loss of a dearly loved person, you might know someone who has, or you wonder how to relate to a person who is in emotional turmoil or feels disoriented because dark clouds of grief cover the mind. While my marriage was not perfect, I am grateful that I could experience a harmonic and fulfilling marriage love relationship with my wife. Others have experienced more difficult and challenging partnerships. On top of the turmoil that shakes the life of any person who has lost a life partner, there are additional unresolved conflicts that burden the grieving person. There might be wounds that have never been processed or forgiven. Perhaps there are feelings of guilt, but now the partner is no longer alive to talk to their spouse and deal with it together. The story I share is my story and reflects my personal experience of dealing with the harshness of loss and grief, and yet I believe that there are numerous areas of common ground that resonate with those who go through the valley of death and mourn the loss of a person they love.

    I wrote this book because writing and reading connect those of us going through similar experiences and struggling with all the uncertainties and fears that often accompany significant loss. Being aware that we are not alone decreases our sense of isolation. Instead of being crushed by the sadness of our grief, listening to another's story of hope can be like "singing on a boat during a terrible storm at sea. You can't stop the raging storm, but singing can change the hearts and spirits of the people who are together on that ship."[4] So I invite you to listen to the melody of my story. It is a story for everyone who has ever lost a loved one and lost themselves a little in the process. You are not alone!

---

4. Lamott, *Bird by Bird*, 237.

Acknowledgments

A BOOK LIKE THIS cannot be written without the feedback, input, encouragement, and help of numerous people. All those who repeatedly heard my story and shared their stories of loss and grief helped me grow in my own understanding of what I experience. Thank you for the time you spent with me and for your openness to listen attentively. This investment in what it means to be human creates a precious fellowship that reveals that there is a blessing in the community of those who grieve and are willing to share some of their ups and downs. It also enabled me to see that I am not alone in this journey.

I am particularly grateful for the insightful thoughts and encouraging responses I have received from my family and friends. My sisters, Jutta and Bettina, stood at my side and made me realize the enormous blessing of having siblings and family. In the peacefulness of your house, Jutta, the process of writing this book significantly advanced. My wonderful parents in law, Uli and Uschi, have lovingly supported me and my children throughout the years in so many ways. Their beautiful house continues to be a precious place of refuge for all of us. We will always stick together! My sons, Jonathan, Florian, and Daniel, have been a source of strength in the process of reflection, and subsequently in the writing and rewriting of my thoughts. Your input has put some details into more accurate focus, and your feedback has improved the wording of important sections, for which I thank you. Even more importantly, your willingness and openness to let me share my story with others, which has made you more vulnerable with your own story of loss and grief of the same person we both love, is a courageous and gracious act. I appreciate it beyond words.

A special thanks goes to Audrey Andersson, a fellow traveler in grief and loss. Your repeated encouragement to continue to write and your persistence to complete the long journey of putting my thoughts into words has made a huge difference, and your expertise of the English language has significantly improved the readability of the final product.

I want to thank the editor of Cascade Books, Michael Thompson, for his initial interest in my manuscript, as well as Matt Wimer, the managing editor of Wipf and Stock Publishers, and George Callihan, the editorial administrative assistant, and their entire team for all their excellent help in making this book available in a timely manner.

This book is written for all the heroes of my heart, who suffer significant loss and who in affliction courageously stand their ground while everything around them is ferociously shaking. I do not see myself as a hero at all. It is rather the unexpected kindness of other people and ultimately God's incredible grace that helped me endure in the dark valleys of grief rather than to succumb to those sinister moments of discouragement. In the experience of loss and grief there are so many things that largely go unnoticed by human eyes but that deserve to be recognized and remembered. The story that is told in this book wants to do just this: recognize and remember what it means to lose a person you love.

Falling

My love,
My longing,
My entire part,

They fall—

Abysmal deep.
Into your arms,
Into your heart.

Frank M. Hasel
December 20, 2021[1]

---

1. The first version of this love poem was written for me by Ulrike on June 3, 1988, just a few days before we got married. Her original words in German were: "*Mein Glück, mein Sehnen, mein Schmerz, sie fallen—nicht ins bodenlose, weich, in Deine Arme, in Dein Herz.*" "My happiness, my longing, my pain—they fall, not rock bottom deep, but soft, into your arms, into your heart." I have slightly edited her words to reflect the abysmal deep feeling of grief.

Chapter 1

Dealing With the Unspeakable

WHAT WORDS CAN DESCRIBE what cannot be explained? How do you tell a person who has never fallen in love how it feels to be deeply in love? If someone asked me a couple of years ago what it was like to lose my mother, I would have responded by saying, "I saw my grandmother die." But now I know it is not quite the same. In fact, it is very different. It seems that the most beautiful and the most painful experiences in life cannot adequately be described with words nor can they be fully fathomed. Every hardship and every tragedy have something about them that defies simple explanations. Just as with joy and beauty, every suffering, every pain, and every significant loss in life is unique. It is as matchless and incomparable as the love we felt for this particular person. We all experience the agony of loss differently because every person is one of a kind and the loving relationship we form with this human being is unique and irreplaceable. Therefore, our grief is ferociously individual, and each person's suffering has its own distinctive qualities.

Losing a person you love deeply is a tough road to walk. It is the stuff of nightmares. I cannot provide an answer to all the questions that come to mind, and I won't even attempt to. What I can do is share a small part of my own story of loss and grief. I used to think that the story of losing my wife was a liability. It is often awkward meeting people who do not know what to say when they hear what happened. People feel sorry for me. Losing the love of your life is not something that is attractive. Being a widower made me feel that I didn't fit into familiar social groups anymore. But over time I realized that my story is an asset. Sharing what happened to me is particularly effective in connecting with other people across time and space who have gone through similar experiences.

Much of what we learn in life comes to us in the form of stories. It has been said that "story, after all, is the vehicle through which we think, imagine, build relationships, make sense of our experiences, and form our identities."[1] Stories are like a compass through which we navigate our lives. Stories appeal to us in vivid ways. They touch our hearts—and minds. They have the power to get through to us in ways that an abstract truth can never achieve. Stories, especially when they are stories about what really took place, have the aroma of truth, and the best stories are told not to escape our world but to better prepare us for living in the world. The fascination of a true story is that you know that it tells how tangible people have acted in difficult and seemingly impossible circumstances. That shapes our imagination and creates credibility and hope. Stories express something distinctly human that distinguishes us from the animal world. The quest to find meaning through stories is an important and uniquely human experience.[2] We tell stories in order to live. That's why there is a hunger for a story in all of us. Stories allow us to connect with the storyteller with greater ease. I hope that sharing my story will create such a bridge that will enable you to cross your valley of grief and will resonate with your unique experience.

My story has become a melody in my own heart that I can share with my children—and the children of my children—and with you. But there is more to my story than just sharing my experience or ordering my thoughts into a coherent, manageable account. In telling my story I also affirm the life of the person I lost: my faithful companion in life, my very best friend, my lover, my confidant, my wife, and the mother of our sons—Ulrike.[3] In a way, telling my story moves my grief forward, expresses my tender love and profound gratitude for her, and so contributes to my healing. Sharing my story with all its fears and panics, sharing what saved my day, sharing what made me move forward and helped me to learn that there is life to be enjoyed even after death is my gift to you.

We may impress people with our strengths, but we connect with them through our vulnerabilities. Dealing with hard experiences in our vulnerability arouses in us an instinctive desire for authenticity. What I share with

---

1. Edelman, *AfterGrief,* 141.
2. Edelman, *AfterGrief,* 142.
3. The English phonetic spelling of Ulrike is: ool-ree-keh.

Dealing With the Unspeakable

you in this book has grown out of my exposure to significant loss and is fiercely honest. This is not a self-help manual or offering a panacea for loss. It is not even offering good advice, although you may find principles that you can apply. In sharing my story, I am not idealizing grief and loss. I do not make pain appear glorious. Losing your life partner is really as bad as you think it is. Probably even worse. In what I write I might even subvert some obvious expectations. If there is one thing that my experience of the harsh reality of losing my wife has taught me, it is to never take things for granted. When you lose a loved person with whom you have shared every facet of your life, the very foundation of your security is violently shaken. It is like a major earthquake. Things that once were familiar become like a foreign and far-off land that is desert-like and hostile. We become painfully aware of the fragility of all human existence. We wonder whether life is still worth living—alone. This can easily make us fearful, even paranoid. The shaking of our security undoubtedly leads to difficult and often nagging questions about life, God, and the meaning of death and justice in this world. These tough questions defy easy answers. No wonder our grieving often creates feelings and thoughts that are frequently incomprehensibly contradictory and deeply confusing. Grief and joy are sometimes close partners on this journey, just like many other emotions and feelings that affect our souls.

Anna Seghers, alias Anna Reiling, the acclaimed Jewish German writer who escaped Nazi controlled territory through wartime France, was notable for exploring and depicting the moral experience of the Second World War. She is reported to have said that a writer needs some fifteen years of distance before they can narrate and tell the story of important events in literary form.[4] As I write this book fifteen years have not yet fully passed for me. I began writing several months after my wife died. It has continued—with interruptions—for more than twelve years. What you read is not the silver bullet that solves every problem. It is not the final word on things. It is more of a snapshot in time, that reflects my current thinking. My thoughts have matured and developed over the years. Yes, Ulrike is no longer alive in person, and yet she is still very much alive in my thoughts and memories. The past years have helped to sufficiently ripen my thoughts to the place where I feel ready to share them in writing. I don't know whether I will ever be able to fully come to grips with what happened when she died. But writing down some significant aspects of my story and reflecting on what

---

4. As quoted in Schubert, *Vom Aufstehen*, 26.

this loss means for me, how it has impacted my life, how it has shaped my identity, and how faith in God has been a source of strength that helped me be resilient in this unpredictable journey, is worth trying.

Fellowship of Grief

There is a certain fellowship in loss into which we are drawn when we experience it. It can be a relief to discover that the aches we think are ours alone are also felt by so many others. It seems that all sorrows can be borne more easily when we put them into a story or tell a story about them.[5] In sharing our stories we articulate that our loved ones matter and we honor them. Talking about them is so important for our healing. In this sense, my story can function like a magnifying glass. It focuses on seemingly small things that are unique to Ulrike and my relationship with her, yet nevertheless are quite significant because they express something universal. In pinpointing details that easily go undetected, my story touches on things we all have in common because of our corporate humanity. I hope that reading my story will spark some courage that enables you to wrestle with your questions and challenges with new vigor. Perhaps you will see the world and yourself with new eyes. Maybe it will ease the way so that you can see that it is all right to cry, that it is all right to turn to others for help, that it is all right to be confused and not to know what to do, that it is perfectly normal to have feelings of envy and anger, that it is all right to be scared of living without the person you love so much, not knowing how to master the future alone. And it is all right to see that there are still moments of light and hope, of unexpected support and encouragement. There are glimpses of faith. These precious parts of the story need to be told as well and deserve to be shared.

My story does not deny the incomprehensible reality of bad things that happen even to very good people. I am convinced we need to learn to live with the unexplainable and we must endure unanswered questions for which there are no easy explanations. The story of my journey is a work in progress. New insights and new encounters with other people will continue to influence my thinking and shape my outlook on life. As incomplete and provisionary as my perspective in this ongoing life experience is, I hope that my story can expand your horizon or can deepen, even a tiny bit, your sense that life is worth living, so restoring buoyancy in dealing with the

---

5. "living_through_loss," September 9, 2021.

harsh realities of loss. May it inspire you to find the courage to carry on as you face tragedy and loss in your own life.

As simple and as complicated and contradictory as this might sound, life is still beautiful and worth living even after horrific things happen in this twisted and imperfect world. May the journey I share with you help you to reflect on your life's journey and may it encourage you to make some healing choices that can help to live your life, knowing that there are people you love—and ever will love!

Being Confronted with Death and Suffering

For many years I was never confronted with severe suffering or death. I experienced a carefree childhood. My life was not perfect, but I was happy. Life does not have to be perfect to be beautiful. I enjoyed the comfort and love of family and friends who enabled me to live successfully. I enjoyed our happy marriage, we had three beautiful and gifted sons, I worked as a pastor and was able to get a PhD in theological studies. I had a satisfying academic career and was the dean of a theological seminary. Life was good. I was content. This changed when I was confronted with a significant loss in 2009. The death of my wife swirled my life around like a tornado. It completely changed my existence. Death often occurs unexpectedly, and frequently much too early. Ulrike was forty-three years old when she was diagnosed with breast cancer. It was the most aggressive form of breast cancer.[6] She did not choose to have cancer. In fact, none of us wanted it. Ulrike had a bright future ahead of her. She was still very much needed. Ulrike had chosen to be a homemaker while our three sons, Jonathan, Florian, and Daniel, were young. She had recently gone back to her career as an elementary teacher, a profession she loved. As a teacher, she was not only very successful but also greatly loved and appreciated by the children she taught. She was highly respected by her peers. We all loved her immensely. But less than a year after she was diagnosed with cancer she died. Those who knew her can testify that she was an amazingly positive and cheerful person. She was an inspiring example of genuine kindness and self-sacrificing love. Ulrike had a living relationship with Jesus and showed unwavering trust in God. When she died, she was at peace with herself, the people she knew, and God. For her, death was a release from all her suffering. For our three children and me it was—and still is—a very cruel loss.

6. The technical name of it is "triple-negative breast cancer."

Love Is!

Mascha Kaléko, one of my favorite poets, lamented the death of her son and in one of her poems wrote:

> The fear of my own death is not that strong,
> it's just the deaths of those who I adore.
> How shall I live when they are here no more? . . .
> He knows it well who can identify;—
> And those enduring it may please forgive.
> Just think: one's own death one just has to die,
> but with the death of others one must live.[7]

Yes, I could face my death, I was not afraid to die. But living with the death of Ulrike, whose pleasant voice filled my former days and made me feel at home, whom I trusted most and who was closest to my heart, is something I am still learning to do. It seems to be a lifelong learning experience for me. Finding new ways to live with the absence of the very person that meant so much to me is a steep and tough learning experience. Confronting the reality of death, facing the experience of living without her, and finding new ways of arranging my life without the person I loved so completely, require courage. Courage is best experienced in the company of others. Even though the experience of the loss I felt is unique, I am not the only person who suffers the loss of a loved one. Recognizing that I am not alone was a small light in the darkness that surrounded me. It was the beginning of a journey that brought healing to my memory. Join me on my journey. Here is how it all began.

---

7. This wonderful English translation of Kaléko's poem "Memento" is found in Nolte, *Poems*, 101. The original German words are printed in the same book, 100: "*Vor meinem eignen Tod ist mir nicht bang, nur vor dem Tode derer, die mir nah sind. Wie soll ich leben, wenn sie nicht mehr da sind? . . . Bedenkt: den eignen Tod, den stirbt man nur, doch mit dem Tod der andern muss man leben*." The German text is also published in Kaléko, *Verse*, 9.

Chapter 2

Tragic Events Often Start Unexpectedly

IT ALL STARTED ON a perfectly normal day. I think it was a Friday in October 2008. Now, I can't even recall the exact day when it all began. Pain often has an element of "blank," where we cannot recollect when it all began. I think it was Friday, October 17. On Sunday I was conducting the wedding of two of my students and it was on that Sunday that Ulrike shared the news with my sister, who was a close friend, and a guest at the wedding. Now, I can only remember that it was a perfectly normal day when it happened. Tragic events often unfold rather unexpectedly and arise out of quite normal circumstances. This makes their dramatic impact on us so life-changing. That morning, Ulrike asked me to feel her right breast as she noticed something different. If something troubled either of us, we would always share it with the other one. I could sense that she needed my support and assurance. Could I feel anything? As I gently probed and felt her breast, I thought maybe there was something there, but I wasn't sure. I held her, hugged her tightly, and tried to reassure her. It really didn't feel like there was anything there. Probably nothing to worry about, but if she was worried, I encouraged her to follow up on it. She was worried and made an appointment with the doctor to check it out. She asked me to come with her to get the results just in case her fears turned out to be reality. A few days later we sat together in the doctor's waiting room. Waiting at a doctor's office is an exercise of patience. At this moment we had no idea that over the next year we would face an increasing number of doctors' appointments, countless medical exams, new treatments, and numerous consultations with various medical experts that confronted us with confusing, unfamiliar words and unhappy news. Where did we spend considerable time waiting for the next steps to unfold in this family saga with a for us yet unknown ending—in doctors' waiting rooms!

A waiting room is an architectural construct whose sole purpose is to provide a space for people whose life is on pause. They are waiting to discover which direction they will take. Will they hear good news or bad? Time and again I am amazed at how carelessly many waiting rooms are designed and how thoughtlessly they are furnished and decorated. In moments when we are most receptive to encouragement or some other positive and uplifting thoughts, there is often very little inspiration in many waiting rooms. What a wasted opportunity to foster hope or to provide some positive inspiration when we need it most.

Eventually, it was Ulrike's turn for her ultrasound. When she came out, I could tell that the news was not good. I squeezed her hand tightly as we walked downstairs to where we had parked our car. The privacy of the car provided an intimate space to talk. As I put my arm around her and held her hand, she shared more details of the results of the ultrasound diagnosis. In her soft voice, I could sense her trembling heart and we began to process the news together. It looked like she had a small tumor in her right breast. More detailed tests with a radiology specialist were required. These new examinations had to be arranged and a new appointment with a specialist was made several days later. In the meantime, we had to learn to wait.

Chapter 3

Diagnosis

Learning to Wait

NO ONE CAN COMPLETELY understand the full impact on you of being told that you have cancer. Cancer, for all the medical progress that has been made in recent years, is still a life-threatening disease. It is still potentially terminal. Suddenly, literally from one moment to the next, out of the blue, we were confronted with the reality of an illness over which we had no control. The thought that this was something that could seriously harm Ulrike's health and even threaten her life rattled and shook the foundation of everything I had taken for granted: life itself. It was not that I was unaware of the fragility of all human life. For me, life is a gift that we receive from God and gratefully cherish. I knew that everything eventually would come to an end. I am an ordained pastor. I have conducted many funerals. I was fully aware that human life will end in death. But to be confronted with such a life-threatening reality in my immediate circle of close friends (yes, my wife was my very best, my closest friend!) made me realize even more fully that life cannot be taken for granted. Being confronted by the vulnerability of life shook the secure footing of the obvious, the things that I had simply assumed as a given. All kinds of thoughts began flooding my mind. Ulrike's cancer diagnosis forced me to face my mortality. It forced me to acknowledge that the reality of death is not some remote moment in the far distant future but can affect me and my immediate family much sooner than anticipated. Death does not always happen in chronological order. The certainty of all our plans came abruptly to a halt. My focus on life got redirected. I began losing a definite focus altogether. I could not fully fathom what I heard the doctor say. That my healthy and happy wife, the love of my life, should have a dangerous and even life-threatening cancer tumor sounded so surreal. My first response was denial: this cannot be true. This simply cannot be! And yet this was exactly what we were abruptly and rudely forced to face. But until more detailed tests were conducted, and those results were confirmed, we did not know for sure. So, we continued to hope for the best—and inwardly I continued to fear the worst. In situations like this both—hope and fear—coexist. In the meantime, time passes, and life goes on somehow. And we wait.

And we continue to wait. That is, I had to learn to wait. To be honest, waiting does not come easy for me.[1] Waiting is not something that is a natural part of me. I hate waiting. I don't like long lines, traffic jams, or delayed appointments. I get frustrated by tardy people and by processes that take longer than necessary. I usually want to get things done swiftly and in the most efficient way possible. Waiting often seems like nothing more than a meaningless delay, literally a waste of time. But there is no human life without waiting. From birth to death, our lives are characterized by waiting. Sometimes the waiting is brief, and time passes quickly. Other times, the waiting lingers for years. Because human beings exist in time, waiting is part of our identity, our story, and our history. There is no historical succession without waiting. The person who lives—waits! The person who waits—lives!

Waiting reminds me that often the things that are most essential and precious to us are the very things that are beyond our power and control. So, we are forced to wait. While we are waiting, the temptation is to be passive—doing nothing, hoping that an unpleasant situation will somehow disappear. Sometimes, the temptation is to focus on the very things we don't have. However, waiting is not just about what we are hoping for in the future. Biblically speaking, waiting is just as much about who we become as we wait. The decisive thing is not what happens to us, but *how* we relate to what happens to us. How we react to what we experience determines how we live and who we are. Waiting always presents us with a spiritual choice: will I allow myself to become impatient and negative while waiting, perhaps even questioning God's goodness in what I experience, or will

---

1. I have described my experience with waiting and some other practical aspects and blessings that come with it in Hasel, *Living for God*, 36–44.

Diagnosis

I embrace the unique opportunity to grow my character and become the person I would never be, without the experience of waiting?

For Ulrike and me this was just the start of many long hours, and even longer days, weeks, and months of waiting. Waiting for new results. Waiting and hoping that things would turn out well, that we would get new appointments in time, that the doctors would be able to help, and that the treatments would cure her. Perhaps the most challenging factor in times of waiting is the uncertainty with which we are confronted. It is hard to live with the uncertainty generated by prolonged periods of waiting. Not knowing what the results will reveal is difficult to endure. Not knowing whether this sickness is serious or not leaves us in limbo. Not knowing what the future holds can drain our energies. Not having any control over the things that are most precious to us makes us nervous. Not knowing how we will be able to cope with the additional stress, the medical bills, the limitations of personal freedom, and the restrictions to do the very things we liked to do creates uncertainty. Not knowing whether we will be able to continue to do some things we enjoyed to do instills some fear. Not knowing how long this will last is a test of our endurance and patience. Not knowing if Ulrike would be healed or if she might die challenged my faith. There were myriads of things I simply did not know. All these unspoken thoughts circled in my mind. Such ideas were confusing. They were draining. They made me feel exhausted and tired. They robbed me of my energy. And yet, they demanded to be dealt with.

At times it all appeared like a bad dream, a nightmare, to me. But it wasn't a dream. It was the harsh reality, a living nightmare, to which we awoke quite abruptly. This waiting—as painful and as unwanted as it is—made me also realize that at least, as long as I am waiting, I am still alive. For this, I am deeply grateful. After all, life in the fellowship of a loving family and good friends is beautiful. However, at the same time, I had to deal with those creeping fears that would intrude on my thoughts and threaten to paralyze me.

Dealing with Creeping Fears

Waiting with uncertainty looming over your head like a dark cloud produces fear. Fear grows to *Angst*. It paralyzes. It fogs our thinking. Acting out of fear is rarely helpful. When we found out that Ulrike had cancer, we were determined not to let fear dominate our thinking. We wanted to do everything in our power to deal with her cancer in the most effective and best way possible. This requires a clear head. But cancer is not a glorious battle that is won easily or quickly. We soon realized that cancer was something beyond our control. The uncertainty of not knowing 100 percent how things would turn out, in the end, at times was unnerving. It certainly drained our emotional and physical energies in unexpected ways. It also allowed us to learn to trust God more fully. After all, we don't know the future, but God does. We cannot tell the end from the beginning. But we can learn to trust the One who knows. We realized that better than knowing all the details of our future was to put our hands into the hand of him who knows the future. Minnie Louise Haskins (1875–1957)[2] has described this so beautifully in her poem "The Gate of the Year." The words of her poem touched the hearts and minds of countless listeners when King George VI quoted from it in his Christmas address on December 25, 1939, at a time when dark clouds loomed over Europe, and indeed the whole world was at the brink of another terrible war:

> And I said to the man who stood at the gate of the year:
> "Give me a light that I may tread safely into the unknown."
> And he replied:
>> "Go out into the darkness and put your hand into the Hand of God.
>> That shall be to you better than light and safer than a known way."
>
> So I went forth, and finding the Hand of God, trod gladly into the night.
> And He led me towards the hills and the breaking of day in the lone East.
>
> So heart be still:
> What need our little life
> Our human life to know,
> If God hath comprehension?
> In all the dizzy strife
> Of things both high and low,
> God hideth His intention.
>
> God knows. His will
> Is best. The stretch of years
> Which wind ahead, so dim
> To our imperfect vision,
> Are clear to God. Our fears
> Are premature; In Him,
> All time hath full provision.[3]

2. On Minnie Louise Haskins see Donnelly, "Gate of the Year."
3. The full text of Haskins's poem can be found at Wikipedia, "Gate of the Year."

Diagnosis

Yes, knowing God was better for me than the light that would illumine our way. Knowing God let us trust him more fully and made us love him for who he is, a compassionate God, who cares for our well-being, who is tender in his love for us, longing to help and eager to redeem. Knowing God for who he really is was better than knowing what was familiar to me. More important than knowing *where* he leads me is *who* leads me!

With God's help, we wanted to face this life-threatening disease that shook us to the core with hope, even though we did not know how it would end. Knowing that God knows the end and he is at our side made us calmer. Even though we could not see God, we trusted that he was with us. This gave us the freedom to confront the unknown with courage and as much realism as possible. Simply ignoring Ulrike's cancer was not an option for us. To be paralyzed by anxiety and fear was not desirable either. Even though we strongly believed in God, his omnipotence, ability, and willingness to help and heal, still some fearful thoughts were circling in our minds. This is a normal human response. Anything out of the ordinary naturally raises legitimate concerns in all of us. It would be strange indeed if fearful thoughts were completely absent in times of life-threatening news. Such fear is not wrong. But fear can easily create a "fertile soil for a new set of fears that have the power to shape the way you interpret and live your life."[4] Often the level of fear we experience when we are confronted with bleak news or when we experience great uncertainty is not just the result of the magnitude we suffer. It has to do with our thoughts and how we view our difficulties. Perhaps even more significant than the unpleasant things with which we are confronted is the way we respond to them and how we react. When fear begins to kidnap our plans and our thoughts begin to circle just around the bad things that happened to us or that could happen to us, our ideas become controlled by devastating negativity. The more we focus on the things we dread, the bigger, and more complicated and insurmountable they become. Usually, decisions we make out of fear tend to be decisions we later regret. Why? Because when fear rules our thinking, we don't see or think about life accurately anymore. Our perspective is severely restricted and distorted.

Ulrike and I talked about the prospect of her illness, and we made the deliberate decision to face the reality of her cancer not through the lens of fear. Instead, we would deal with it in informed ways, tackling it through the lens of faith and hope. This meant encouraging each other to focus on

---

4. Tripp, *Suffering*, 59.

God and his character,[5] rather than on our problems. It also meant, among many other things, that we tried to find the best evidence-based medical advice available. This information is not easily found on the Internet. You need to know where and how to search for it. Google algorithms and those of other search engines are not programmed to lead you into truth, but they lead you to those websites that receive the greatest attention and bring the biggest financial gain. Sometimes this enhanced our fears. We were fortunate to have several friends who are excellent medical doctors, experts whom we trusted, and whom we could turn to for a second opinion. We also were glad that, as a patient, my wife always had the right to get a second opinion! At times it was simply helpful as they could explain to us some of the technical medical jargon that came along with every new test result and treatment. We quickly realized that in the heat of the moment and the shortness of time in our brief interactions with the doctors we often forgot to ask about certain things. Having our questions written down helped us to address the things that were important to us and to receive the information we needed to make informed decisions. When we knew that we would have an important meeting with the doctors who were treating Ulrike, or when we had to decide on new therapies and the next steps that needed to be taken, we tried to write down some of our questions ahead of time. We found it helpful to ask what our options were for a certain treatment or medication. What would be the best possible outcome that could be expected, if we were to pursue this, and what were the worst results? What would we gain? What would we lose? If the doctor with whom we consulted allowed for a more personal question we asked for his or her honest, personal opinion, and what he or she would do if they found themselves in our place. What would they decide and why?

The interaction with some medical doctors was challenging. Especially when we encountered medical doctors who behaved like "demigods in white coats." I often wondered if they are aware that their words become key chapters in the stories of their patients and the patient's families with whom they interact! Some did not hesitate to let us know in rather uncompromising words that we were not medical experts when we wanted to understand some things more fully and raised some questions. Unfortunately, our experience was that many medical people often have insufficient time for questions and even less time to actually listen attentively to what was on our hearts and minds. A good doctor is not just competent in their area

---

5. For some practical ideas on how to do this see Hasel, *Longing for God*, 94–97.

of expertise, but they can also skillfully interact with patients who need help and who are often in a state of shock, especially if they have received a potentially life-threatening diagnosis. Fortunately, we were blessed with several doctors who were exceptionally kind, very helpful, and competent! Seeking a second and informed opinion on significant decisions we had to make was always positive and helpful. Gathering such information did not eliminate all our fears. However, it certainly helped us to tackle some things more confidently and in an informed manner, that was not driven by fear but by the hope that Ulrike would receive the best possible treatment and would be helped and healed.

Coping with Ever-Changing Circumstances

In the meantime, life went on and we had to find flexible ways to cope with and adapt to ever-changing circumstances, dealing with new situations that we had never confronted before. For me, this meant that I had to creatively integrate the time and energy for these new appointments and decision-making processes into a full-time teaching load. Ulrike had to do the same. We had to find new ways to deal with this emerging situation. We had to learn to share and talk about our fears together. In time we would tell our sons, families, and the wider community, but first, we had to develop ways of being open about what was happening. We talked honestly about the risk of losing her in this battle. We had to find ways to deal with the uncertainties of the future and commit our anxiety and our lives into God's hands and trust his faithfulness.

I am grateful for Ulrike's wisdom and creativity. She instinctively knew how important it is to celebrate the little successes in moments of uncertainty. She found ways to acknowledge things that went well. She was creative in finding micro-vacation moments that created memories that no one can steal and that bound us together. This attentiveness to things that brightened our day made the quality of our life so much better. She understood more fully than any of us how serious her condition was. She intuitively knew that a new phase in our lives had begun. It would require extraordinary dedication and she needed my unwavering support and help.

She suggested we recognize this new stage of our journey by buying new wristwatches to remind us that time is precious and fleeting and that it is the meaningful moments together that count. I still remember the special moment when we bought our watches. For me, this watch is still a visible reminder that the fleeting moments of our lives are in God's gracious hands.

But it was not just all about us as a married couple. Our children needed our attention. Their lives were affected by Ulrike's cancer as well. Ulrike needed support and encouragement and I felt responsible to support her emotionally and spiritually as best as I could. It is not only the person who is struggling with cancer who needs support. The support person—often the spouse—as well as the family members of the cancer patient also need support. I often felt inadequate to provide the support that I felt Ulrike needed and that I wanted to give. On more than one occasion this made me face the unpleasant reality of my deficiencies and shortcomings. I guess this is something that every support person feels in some way or another. I am grateful for close friends and colleagues who were incredibly understanding and backed me up and took over some of my responsibilities so that I could be more flexible and available for Ulrike. I am also grateful that God knows all my deficiencies and mistakes and generously and freely forgives me and carries me in his sustaining grace. We all need his grace and I, perhaps, needed it the most.

Somehow, during this constantly changing situation, our daily family life routine had to continue. Yet with every new doctor's appointment and every new step in the protracted treatment process, there were still more telephone calls, more texts, and more emails that needed to be written, which in turn generated even more incoming phone calls demanding our attention. There was a myriad of decision-making processes that resulted in planning, rearranging, and canceling our schedules. We had to tell our friends and family, our work colleagues, church members, and students. But more than that was needed.

How to Share the News with Others?

Ulrike and I needed to find creative ways to help us deal with the situation so that life was manageable. We wanted to feel somewhat comfortable in how we handled things, not pressured and stressed by the circumstances we found ourselves in. This is easier said than done. Our challenge was intensified because both of us were public figures in our community. Ulrike was a respected elementary school teacher. She had successfully taught at a private church school for many years and just recently had begun a new job teaching grades one to four at a public elementary school in the

Diagnosis

neighboring town of Julbach, Germany, not far from where we lived. I was a theology teacher and dean of the theology department at Bogenhofen, a college in Austria. Both of us were active church members in our local congregation. We were well-known in our communities and far beyond. How do you deal with the need for privacy when you are confronted with the news that your wife has cancer? How do you balance that with people who know you wanting to know what is going on and how you are doing? We first shared the news only with our immediate family and a small circle of very good and trusted friends. To suffer the effects of an illness like cancer, over which you have no control, and which makes you feel vulnerable, is so personal, so private, so intimate, that we did not want to share it with the "whole world." We just wanted our closest family members and best friends to know. We wanted them to pray with us and for us. We needed their emotional and practical support! Our families turned out to be a real blessing on the journey that was ahead of us.

Once the initial results were confirmed and we knew that Ulrike would need surgery it became obvious that we could not keep this a secret. Soon others found out because she was missing work due to her surgery. I accompanied her to many new doctors' appointments, and I visited her at the hospital, as often as I could. People began to sense that something was wrong, something out of the ordinary was happening. But how do you handle such a situation? How do you share such news? Do you want to share it at all? Or do you rather try to keep it a secret for as long as possible? How do you maintain your privacy? How do you keep the balance between not isolating yourself from the community that might give you strength and yet not becoming as transparent as a fish tank, where everyone sees and knows everything, and nothing is hidden? In a small community, where everyone knows everyone, it is difficult to keep a secret. Yet, some things are so private and personal that you do not want to share them with everybody. Everyone needs to find a way with which they are comfortable.

The news that Ulrike had cancer spread like wildfire. I quickly realized it is virtually impossible to escape the intensity of other people's curiosity. Soon we had to deal with incoming phone calls from friends, curious church members, as well as faculty and staff at the schools. We had to respond to increasing numbers of emails and text messages from people far and near. Every time we had to repeat the same story, give the same update, and explain we did not know how everything would end. Not only was this emotionally and physically extremely draining, but now we were confronted with an additional challenge. We did not just have to deal with our uncertainties and many questions, we often had to deal with other people's reactions and questions on top of everything else. This quickly became very exhausting. With all the other uncertainties lingering over us, we did not have the energy and power to share even small pieces of information with everybody who happened to have heard the news. We realized that not everybody was as sensitive to our needs as would be desirable. Some people were simply curious, and some were just nosy. We had to deal with all of them and we wanted to treat them kindly. I am not sure if we succeeded in this.

It became increasingly clear to us that because of our public roles in our communities, we felt that people needed to be kept informed of what was happening. For us, we decided the best way to handle this was to share regular updates and information about our situation with two very close and trusted friends. They knew us well and often sensed, without having to say much, how we were doing. These two trusted friends received crucial updates on new developments from us every week or so and then shared them with whoever wanted to get an update. We told church members and the people at the school where I worked that they could contact one of those two people for further updates. We kindly asked that all others would refrain from contacting us and this helped us enormously in maintaining our privacy. It also significantly saved our much-needed emotional and physical energy. It lowered the number of incoming phone calls considerably and helped us to focus our attention on things that were important for our survival. We still spent substantial time talking and communicating with our immediate families and those whom we felt were supportive of our immediate needs.

Chapter 4

Facing the Unknown

Dealing with "Good" Advice

Learning to share part of our story with others in a guarded way was one thing. Dealing with the flood of "good" advice on healthful living from well-meaning people is a completely different ballgame. It did not take long before we were bombarded with all kinds of amazing recipes, extraordinary medicines, or spectacular remedies that people had heard about or firmly believed in. They all meant well. These special cures and cancer antidotes allegedly were able to do quite miraculous things to restore one's health and kill cancer cells. We listened. We looked for information from experts in the field and double-checked extraordinary claims as best as we could. Again, this took time and energy. Sometimes, even after careful and painstaking research, we still were not fully convinced about what we were told, or we were uncertain about the effectiveness of some of the things that were suggested by others. But the time comes when you need to make decisions because time is short, and time is of the essence when you are dealing with a life-threatening disease. We could not experiment with everything. We simply did not have the time, nor did we have the money to pay for some of these treatments. Most of them were not covered by our regular health insurance. We were willing to try everything that seemed reasonable to us and was supported by credible evidence. We especially did everything that supported and strengthened the immune system and so Ulrike's vitality and health. When you are confronted with such a plethora of different options, where some treatments appear to produce conflicting results, you reach a point where you must decide whom to trust and what therapy you want to pursue. We were fortunate to have several trusted friends who are trained medical doctors. Being able to ask them, sometimes just sending them an email for advice when we had questions, was a huge blessing. While ultimately it was Ulrike's decision, she usually would consult with me and both of us made a decision together. *We* had to be convinced about how to handle things. *We* had to learn to live with it. In the final analysis, *we* had to feel comfortable with whatever *we* decided to do. *We* needed to support each other. *We* needed to be convinced about the proper treatment *we* wanted to pursue, and *we* needed to decide which way to go. After all, *we* were ultimately responsible for our decisions. In situations like this, if you are not wholeheartedly in support of whatever you do, you will not receive the maximum benefit of whatever therapy you choose. We had to learn not to be offended by the reactions of others when we decided to pursue a different course of action or a different treatment than what certain well-meaning people would have chosen or recommended. Dealing with such reactions was not always easy. Especially if they came from people that were close to us—or who thought they were close to us. We firmly believed that God could heal and could perform a miracle if he in his sovereignty so chose. At the same time, we did not feel it was an indication of a lack of faith to pursue evidence-based medical therapy and to support Ulrike's health and immune system to strengthen her vitality. It was a matter of evidence-based sensibility, common sense, responsible action, and trust in God. To us, these things were not mutually exclusive but belonged together.

Why Did Ulrike Get Cancer?

Throughout her entire life, Ulrike was exemplarily consistent in her healthy lifestyle. She was a woman with a happy and joyful disposition. She enjoyed healthy meals and a balanced plant-based diet. She was an exceptionally talented and creative cook. My wife did not just enjoy preparing healthy meals. What she prepared was a feast for the eyes as well. But even more importantly: what she prepared tasted really delicious. At least most of the time! For us, meals were family highlights, precious moments where we would sit together. We would not just eat but share things that were on our hearts and minds. Eating together was a joyful experience.

Food was not the only thing that made Ulrike radiant and strong. There were so many other things that supported her health. It was a delight to be in her presence. She had a nonthreatening way to engage in meaningful conversations. Ulrike was not just healthy physically; she was an emotionally and spiritually balanced person. She was at peace with herself and at peace with others around her. She loved the outdoors and enjoyed extended walks in the countryside at a lovely nature preserve in our neighborhood. We lived in the middle of a parklike campus with an ancient castle, out in the country. We preferred to live in the more peaceful, relaxed rural setting and were glad that we did not have to live in the hustle and bustle of a big city with its many visual and acoustic distractions.

Ulrike liked to cycle. As a child, she had enjoyed interesting and entertaining bicycle vacations with her family creating precious memories and fascinating stories that she sometimes told us. As a student at the university in Heidelberg, she cycled to the university and to do her grocery shopping. One of the first things we bought as a young married couple were two bicycles. When we were newly married, we moved to the United States, where I did my graduate and postgraduate studies in theology. Ulrike took classes with me and then got a scholarship to pursue her master's in education. In our free time, we explored the countryside and the beautiful rolling hills of the American Midwest on our bicycles rather than having to use the car.

Ulrike had so many talents. She liked to swim and, to me, she was as elegant as a fish in the water. I admired her for this. She liked to sing. She had a beautiful alto voice and could accompany almost any song immediately. In fact, I first got to know her when she attended a youth camp where she was preparing for a concert with a youth choir that she had recently joined.

Ulrike was content. She knew that she was deeply loved—by her parents, by me, by her children, by a few good and close friends, and most of all by Jesus. He was her best friend. Faith in God gave her a sense of purpose and identity. It filled her with hope, and I believe it was the source of her tender love. Ulrike never desired to be center stage. For her, her family was of primary importance. Having successfully completed her master's in education, she was accepted into the doctoral program to pursue a PhD in education. I repeatedly encouraged her to do this because I knew that she had great potential and would succeed. She had always been an A student and, when we took classes together, she often got better grades than I did. For her, a PhD was not the most important achievement. She placed greater value on spending quality time with our children, especially while they were still young and at home. She deliberately invested her precious time and creative energy to homeschool our children. After she had helped to establish a church school in our local community and our children were a little older, she started teaching as an elementary teacher part-time, which she found deeply satisfying.

During her entire life, Ulrike never took drugs, and she was not addicted to any substances. Ulrike never smoked a single cigarette. She practiced a healthy lifestyle. She enjoyed regular exercise. Her positive attitude and joyful disposition contributed to her emotional and physical well-being. She was hopeful in her spiritual walk with God. Her unwavering trust in God's goodness was an inspiring example for all of us. So why did she get cancer?

Some people believe that if you do just the right things God will protect you and no harm will hit you. Ulrike proved those people wrong. I guess many people follow God for the wrong reasons. They just want to be blessed by him. Yes, if we practice a healthy lifestyle and live responsibly, a lot of sicknesses can be avoided and many negative effects on our health can be significantly reduced, and we will enjoy greater health and vitality. We might even live longer than the average population.[1] But ultimately death hits home with everyone. Even the healthiest person, who enjoys a plant-based diet, exercises regularly, and has a living, vibrant faith in God, lives in an imperfect world. We all are affected by the pollution in the water we drink, the air we breathe, and by other poisonous influences in our environment, many of which are man-made. Because we live in a sinful world even Christians are not immune from such negative influences on their health. Even the healthiest people can get sick. Of course, I wondered why this happened to Ulrike. I think it would have been strange if these kinds of questions didn't cross my mind. For us, however, it was not so much the question "*Why her?*" that bothered us and made us think. We created our own set of *why* questions: *why should she not get sick? Why should only other people get cancer? Why should only others suffer? Why should she be exempt if we live in an imperfect world?* This change of perspective helped us to deal with her illness from a broader perspective and enabled us to have empathy with others who suffered a similar plight. It also helped us not to get lost in the vain search for answers to difficult questions for which there are no simple or fully satisfactory explanations.

---

1. See the fascinating article by Buettner, "Secrets of Long Life," 2–26.

When Ulrike found out about her cancer tumor, she started to learn as much as she could about her disease. She wanted to understand what causes cancer and what could be done to stop it. She soon refrained from all sugar and started an even more rigorous healthy diet and exercise program. We supported her as best as we could. We also prayed. We prayed earnestly! It's what you naturally do when you believe in God—and even people who don't cherish a close relationship with God are often inclined to pray in times of dire need. We had great faith in God. Ulrike asked for a special anointing for the sick—twice, once at the beginning of her illness and then toward the end of her ordeal. We tried everything. But less than a year after she was diagnosed with cancer, she died.

Why did she die? I don't know why! I have no satisfying explanation. To live without an answer to agonizing questions is precarious and I found it hard to keep my footing. I had to learn to live with open questions, because on this side of heaven my horizon and my knowledge are limited, and I don't know all the factors that might be involved in this. All I know for sure, and accept by faith, is that I believe that God is good and does not delight in human suffering and pain. Some questions exist in order to be answered. Other questions exist because they want to be lived despite all answers or even without any answers! Learning to live in response to this question and with all kinds of other difficult questions was the real challenge going forward.

Dealing With Regrets

During the short months in which Ulrike battled her aggressive cancer, we went through every conceivable emotional high and low. After her initial treatment and first surgery, we had good hopes to be able to battle her cancer successfully. Unfortunately, our hope was grounded on a fatal mistake. As we found out sometime later, the hospital mixed up the results of the biopsies and gave us a wrong diagnosis. Instead of a hormone-receptor positive tumor, as we were initially told, she had triple-negative breast cancer. This required a very different therapy and treatment. Because of this *faux pas* by the hospital, the swift treatment of her particular cancer was delayed and our trust in the medical practitioners at that particular hospital suffered a significant blow. We decided to transfer Ulrike to another hospital that was recommended to us. We were so fortunate that there was another hospital close enough to where we lived, where we trusted the medical people, and where she received the treatment she needed. Here we experienced highly competent people and the help and personal attention she received made all the difference. Looking back on this incident made me wonder what might have been different if we had received the correct diagnosis and treatment from the very beginning. These kinds of questions are typical, and I faced them repeatedly and in different settings and forms over the course of her illness. These are nagging questions that eat away at your soul if you let them: *What if* we had detected the tumor earlier? *What if* they had not made this careless mistake? *What if* we had opted for a different therapy? *What if* I had been more kind and more caring for Ulrike? *What if* God had intervened and healed her?

What if questions are virtually endless. They cloud our thinking, and they often torment our minds. I didn't find any easy answers to the "what if?" questions at the time. Much of what if, or perhaps, could have happened, remains entirely hypothetical. The reality is what happened can't be changed. Instead, I am forced to deal with the reality that confronts me now. Even if I could have changed things or acted differently, there was no guarantee that the outcome would be different or better. I realized that I had to learn to live with whatever confronts me. When there were situations and circumstances where we could change things, like transferring Ulrike to a different hospital for her treatment and that option was reasonable and within our reach, we took the initiative to change things for the better. When things were beyond our control and could not be rectified, we decided to accept whatever it was and to deal with it positively and constructively. We wanted to do everything in our power to make the best of the situation we found ourselves in. Rather than clinging to a past incident and mulling over hypothetical alternatives, we decided to deal with the reality at hand and make decisions that enabled us to live every day with hope. This was our strategy as we moved forward.

Chapter 5

Hope Frustrated

AFTER ULRIKE HAD UNDERGONE two surgeries at the first hospital and when all other treatment strategies we tried did not bring any improvement in her condition, we could literally see and feel the tumor growing and spreading to different parts of her body. By the end of the year, she was in great pain. Christmas 2008 was a sober and melancholy Christmas for us all. Normally we traveled to my parents-in-law and spent Christmas with them in their cozy house. Instead, we decided to stay at home because Ulrike was unable to travel in her condition.

It became increasingly clear to us that more action was needed, and we decided to start the recommended chemotherapy at the new hospital. Ulrike tolerated the chemotherapy amazingly well. By May 2009 the tumor had shrunk to the point that it could not be seen anymore at the control screenings. It had visibly disappeared, and we were full of hope that she had made it and the cancer was defeated. We were all elated. Her chemotherapy was followed by a series of radiation treatments, and then, we thought, everything was over, and she would be cured. In July we went on a family vacation to Bornholm, a lovely Danish island in the Baltic Sea. We had to cut our vacation short because Ulrike felt increasing pain. When we arrived back in Austria, she was admitted to the hospital immediately. The cancer had returned and spread to her lungs and spine. After a few days and more treatments, they allowed her to return home where we took care of her until her condition deteriorated to the point where she needed more professional medical attention and support. In just a little over one month after we returned from our last family vacation she died.

The Words No One Wants to Hear

I vividly remember the moment I received the news that Ulrike had died. A couple of days earlier she was admitted to the hospital again. Her cancer had spread and affected her lungs, making it increasingly difficult for her to breathe. She needed additional oxygen. Fortunately, my parents-in-law had arrived earlier and helped us with cooking and maintaining the normal routine of running the household as much as possible. This enabled me to visit Ulrike often in the hospital. I did not want to leave her alone. I still remember she died on a Saturday, a Sabbath. In the morning I was with her in the hospital. Our oldest son, Jonathan, had just returned from Guadeloupe, the tiny butterfly-shaped island in the Caribbean, where he had served as a student missionary at a small school for a year. We were so happy that he was with us again. The day before Ulrike had talked with our three sons. She hugged each of them. Although she was already very weak and needed oxygen to support her breathing, she expressed her love for each of them. But this Sabbath morning I was alone with her in the hospital. Later in the morning, when the doctor made her routine medical round, she talked with me privately. She politely asked whether I was aware that the situation with my wife was serious. She was relieved when I told her that we were fully aware that Ulrike might not live very long and could die soon and that we had spoken about her death. She appreciated that we were not ignoring the signals of her declining strength and health and added that she did not think that it was that serious yet. She thought Ulrike was strong enough to live a few more days. She just wanted to make sure that we were fully aware that she would not live much longer and that we did not deny that harsh reality. Her words influenced my decision on how to spend the rest of the day.

This morning I remained alone with Ulrike. She was tired and rather weak. I sat at her bedside and just enjoyed being close to her. After a while, I took her Bible and was quietly leafing through it. Ulrike loved to read her Bible. She had marked many passages and had highlighted several of her favorite Bible verses with different colors. Her comments in the margin revealed how particular passages had become meaningful to her at different stages of her life and in her journey with cancer. As I skimmed through her Bible, I came across one of her favorite texts that had become particularly meaningful to her during the past year. It is found in Ps 27:1 where David writes: *"The Lord is my light and my salvation; whom shall I fear? The Lord is the strength of my life; of whom shall I be afraid?"* (NKJV). As I read the psalm, I must have quietly spoken the words and to my surprise Ulrike suddenly joined in, reciting the beginning of the psalm by heart before she dozed off again. This assured me that she was still fully alert in her mind, even though she did not speak much and could hardly breathe. I sat beside her the whole afternoon. I did not want to leave her alone, and I definitely did not want her to be alone in the final moments of her life. When we got married, I had promised to stay at her side in good days and adversity. I wanted to stay true to my vows, especially as her health was rapidly declining.

Later that Saturday afternoon my parents-in-law arrived with my sons to visit Ulrike. Because the doctor had been so confident that Ulrike was still strong enough to live a couple more days, I decided to drive home with the children and left Ulrike—not alone, but with her parents. When I arrived at home after a thirty-five minute drive my youngest son, Daniel, went outside to play, Jonathan met with some of his friends, and I wanted to take a short nap. My son Florian was with me in the bedroom when the phone rang. It was my brother-in-law, Milan. He had arrived with my sister at the hospital shortly after I had left. Within just a few minutes of their arrival, Ulrike breathed her last and died. Milan had the tough task to inform me.

The phone call with the news of her death came unexpectedly. With the information I had received from the doctor earlier in the morning, I had not anticipated that Ulrike would die so quickly. When I received the news, I instinctively knew what had happened and I howled out such a deep cry of pain as I had never heard before. It was a terrible and heart-wrenching moment. I felt a stabbing pain in my chest. It was like an atomic bomb had detonated silently and devastated my life.

I encountered a strange blend of utter incomprehension, grief, and anger over the situation that I was not present when Ulrike died. I could have easily arranged to be there if I had only known. At the same time, I felt utterly helpless to change anything. My initial reaction was coupled with the experience of deep emotional pain and grief that pierced my heart and soul. There was a strange mix of total disbelief that this should be true. My heart shouted this cannot be true, while at the same time my head knew that it was a reality that could not be debated, and yet it felt so unreal and far off. It made me exceedingly sad and pushed me into a state of shock. Fortunately, I was not completely alone when this happened, and I was able to swiftly find Jonathan and, after some searching, Daniel. Once I shared the sad news with them, we headed back to the hospital where we would see Ulrike again—but this time she was no longer alive. She was dead. Death is devoid of any warmth. When my hand touched her cold body the grim reality of death was undeniable. Knowing death with my mind alone did not have the same conviction as touching her cold and lifeless body.

When I entered the hospital room where she was, I was glad not to be alone. My mother-in-law and my sister, who are both trained nurses, had asked for permission to wash Ulrike and care for her one last time. They had done a beautiful job. I was so glad that my close family was with me in the room. Tears flowed. We hugged each other. We cried. We talked quietly. We could not fully fathom that she was dead and yet it was so clear and indisputable. To see a dead person is a strange and even scary experience. When I saw her, I could tell that life had left Ulrike. The warmth of life was absent. The color of her skin looked paler. She did not breathe anymore. There was no reaction when I touched her skin. She was cold and lifeless. Life is a mystery. What keeps us alive is beyond our fullest human understanding. The end of our life is a mystery too. While her physical body was still there, her consciousness did not exist anymore. She did not participate in what was going on around her. Her breath of life had stopped. The warmth of her living being had changed into a cold, dead body. It seems as if death is the enemy of all life. It is strange and unfamiliar to see a person like this. And it is excruciatingly painful, especially when it is someone we love. It numbed my feelings and ripped them wide open at the same time. What death does to us is utterly unbelievable.

Death Comes as a Surprise

When I received the phone call that told me about Ulrike's death, I immediately knew that she was gone. I knew she was no longer alive. I instinctively knew that she had died. In the middle of life, we are confronted and surrounded by the reality of death. I couldn't fully fathom the dreadful news. Neither could I comprehend my feelings and understand why it had happened so suddenly. Even though I knew theoretically and intellectually that Ulrike would die soon, I was unprepared for the moment of her death. It seems there is always an element of surprise when our life ends. Just as there is a joyous feeling of surprise when new life is born and the newborn baby takes his first own breath, so the last breath that a person breathes signals the sadness of the finality and finitude of our mortal life. In death, our life comes to an end. Death has an irreversible finality about it. Only in the presence of death did I fully realize how much I loved her and how much she meant to me!

It might sound strange, but Ulrike's death happened unexpectedly. I was aware that her strength was declining and that she would not live much longer. Humanly speaking I knew full well that the end of her life was imminent. I had the realistic feeling that she would not survive her cancer. At the same time, I always hoped that somehow a miracle would happen. I did not doubt that God could perform such a miracle, even though humanly speaking that was not to be expected. But that is what miracles are, after all, things out of the ordinary, supernatural occurrences of grace. In my head, I knew that she had only a very short time to live. Yet, her death definitely came too early! Death always comes unexpectedly, even though in some cases you can literally see death looming over a person who is still alive. Even then, the actual end of life comes as a surprise. It was an ordinary day when that moment occurred, and Ulrike's life ended. But that moment made that day extraordinary in its significance for my life and everyone else in my family. It is remarkable when we are confronted with a disaster that we often focus on how unremarkable the circumstances were in which the unthinkable occurred. But now her death had become a reality that affected my life as nothing had ever impacted me before.

Preparing the Funeral

Within hours of Ulrike's death, I had to deal with the grim reality of starting to organize my wife's funeral. For events like this, it is good to have some trusted friends and family around. I was blessed to have had kind, competent people by my side in this complex and emotionally demanding decision-making process. I needed people whom I could trust and who knew both of us well. These decisions needed to be made within a couple of days, but they were far-reaching decisions that needed a clear mind. But my thinking was anything but clear and structured. My mind was like a foggy blur. I did not know what to do with myself. I felt confused. My mind did not function properly. I just could not think clearly or at least not as clearly as I wanted to think. In some ways, everything felt hectic, while simultaneously time seemed to stand still for me. My thoughts were similarly contradictory. All this should not come as a surprise. When you lose a person you love, you are overwhelmed with the strongest emotions you have ever experienced. I felt sad. Extremely sad. In my sadness and trauma of being bereaved, my body and my mind went their separate ways. It felt as if there was a sort of invisible blanket between me and the world, covering my mind and thinking. I found it hard to take in what anyone said. Just then I needed to think clearly. Funerals are quite expensive! I mention this just in case you didn't know! Funerals cost a lot of money. Like most people, we had not saved money for such an occasion. On top of all the emotional turmoil, I was trying to process the added financial challenges of a funeral. There were so many things that needed to be decided and there are just as many things that needed to be paid for.

What cemetery should she be buried in? What spot was available for her grave? What coffin should I choose, or should I opt for a cremation? What flowers should I select to fit in the whole ceremony? Would they reflect my taste and what she liked? Who should I ask to preach the funeral sermon? Who needed to be notified and invited? Where in the world did I have the addresses and contact information for them? What should be printed on the funeral announcement? What words would express what is important to us? What music did I want to be played accompanying the funeral? And who could play the music, the organ, etc.? What public and local authorities needed to be informed? The list of things seemed endless. Without the help of people who were at my side, driving with me to the funeral home, visiting the cemetery, accompanying me at the local authorities, etc., I would have never been able to manage all this by myself. I needed people who were supportive, thoughtful, and considerate, and who would give me some gentle guidance in all these questions, while at the same time not pushing their personal preferences or opinions.

Lonely Decisions

The strangest thing in all this was something I was not really prepared for. Suddenly, I was forced to decide important things more or less by myself. This was a new experience for me. Of course, I had decided things by myself before. But I liked to discuss important decisions with my wife. I valued her input and was immensely interested in her ideas and perspective on things. Before making significant decisions, we discussed things together.

Now I could no longer get her opinion. I could no longer benefit from her insights and expertise. I could no longer share the responsibility for my decision with her. Now I had to make all these decisions, by myself. There were a lot of decisions that needed to be made. I felt very alone. I missed her help. I felt insecure and overwhelmed. This was just the very beginning of my journey with loss and grief.

Chapter 6

Facets and Feelings of Loss and Grief

WHEN ULRIKE DIED, LIFE as I knew and enjoyed it imploded. My life turned upside down on multiple levels. Nothing had prepared me for it. I felt that not only my half of me had died and been torn away, much more was lost. I felt incomplete. It felt as if I was less *me* without her. It felt as if part of *my* life—*the* decisive part of my life!—no longer existed. It felt as if life itself was ripped out of me. Her permanent absence, her death, was like an iron gate that hindered me from proceeding on the mutual path that we had ventured on during our marriage. Ways that we had walked together now were dead ends.

It was not just that I mourned the loss of her at my side. There was an additional sadness, for better or for worse, that had to do with who I was. Her death not only separated us, but it also changed who I was. Without her, I found myself to be a different *me*. I was no longer who I used to be. Perhaps it is like the amputation of one of my legs. I imagine losing a leg is a very painful experience. After a while, the pain of the amputation might get less, although there still is the very real phantom pain that I must deal with. But even if the pain of the amputation might grow less, the amputated leg will never be restored. With the loss of one leg my entire *modus vivendi*, my entire way of living is affected: how I get up and try to get dressed; how I play sports; how I sit down and stand up; how I walk; even how I lay in bed nothing is as it used to be. Many things that I used to enjoy and loved to do with two legs, I can't do anymore. Losing my wife felt like an amputation.

Only worse. The two of us were one. But now, after her death, the one who remains, me, was even less than one, or so it seemed to me.

Even today without her there is a huge hole in my world. In the place where she was, there is *nothing*. Without her there is *emptiness*. There is a vacuum in my life. Only a void remains, or so it feels. The world became darker and drab without her. Her permanent absence is excruciatingly painful to endure. The loss of her physical presence, her input, her creativity, her perspective, her humor, her touch, her smell, and her love, is so irreversibly gone. Death is grimly final in its consequences. It is not just that she is missing from my life. She was an integral part of my life, and it feels as if part of me, the essential part for that matter, is missing with her. Nothing can fill the void that her absence left behind.

Yet, while I acutely felt her loss in my life, it gradually dawned on me that her death is not just my personal loss, but it is her loss as well. She is no longer able to enjoy the bright autumn colors, the sound of her favorite music, or the pleasure of reading a good book. She can no longer walk in the beautiful nature that she loved so much and breathe the crisp air. She can no longer spend time with good friends and family. She can no longer go to church, nor will she be helping with her sons' weddings. She will never have the pleasure of holding a grandchild in her arms. All this and much more she is deprived of. She will never experience any of this anymore. I do not just lament my loss; I grieve what she has lost as well.

To lose a loved one is brutal and extremely cruel. Without her presence and loving support, I felt so vulnerable and naked. This must be the feeling of a broken heart. Indeed, there is some surprising evidence that widows and widowers have a 41 percent higher risk of dying in the three months following the death of their spouse. Their bodies reveal higher levels of inflammation in the bloodstream and lower heart-rate variability, which is an indicator of health risks. Widows and widowers were more likely to have a heart attack or stroke within thirty days of the death of their spouse. They also experience a 20 percent higher level of depression.[1] This is all the result of severe emotional stress. The death of a loved one affects the nervous system and our physical health. Grieving is not just an emotional roller coaster; it has physical repercussions. This just confirms what we all instinctively know, and what poems, lyrics, music, literature, and art have been telling us for years: our hearts really can break when we lose the one we love. Our physical health is at risk and is negatively affected.

---

1. As quoted in Bates, *Languages of Loss*, 50.

But grieving the loss of my wife did so much more to me than just feeling the pain of her absence. It affected how I related to the people around me. I began to see the world around me with different eyes.

Life Did Not End

One of the most shocking and incomprehensible observations I made early in the wake of my loss was that, even though my world had flipped upside down, life around me continued. For me, time stood still, but for everyone around me, life continued, as if nothing had happened. Bills still needed to be paid. The garbage still needed to go out. My sons still needed to go to school. Everyone else lived their lives as if nothing had happened. This disconnect was jarring, added to my irritation, and increased my isolation in grief. I simply could not understand how others would and could continue with their daily routines when for me life was shattered. Especially during the first few weeks and months this feeling often crossed my mind. I remember that shortly after Ulrike's funeral I had to go into town to do some errands. I usually like to do some window shopping, particularly looking at the nice displays of new clothes and other things. I came across one shop which sold beautiful women's clothes. I saw a dress that Ulrike would have liked, and which would have suited her. Suddenly I thought that there was no need for women's clothing stores anymore. I felt as if women's clothes were totally unnecessary. I realize now how stupid and limited my perspective was at that moment, but that is how I felt during those first days. As far as I was concerned, I could not understand why such things were still needed. What increased my pain was the realization that what I had previously enjoyed, like buying a lovely dress for her as a surprise, I could no longer enjoy. At the same time, I realized that life kept on going for other people. I had to learn to live with this reality and find ways to integrate it into my new life without her, which also continues.

Loneliness

Of course, I felt lonely after the death of Ulrike. She was the best friend I ever had. Losing a person you love, losing your spouse, leaves you lonely. Very lonely. The love of my life was missing. Without her, my life had lost its vibrancy. The elixir of her presence was gone. Without Ulrike life was just not the same. This loneliness surfaced in so many different contexts.

Now I cannot snuggle into bed with my best friend and feel the warmth of her skin. Now I cannot talk things over with her anymore. Now I cannot share my joys and sorrows with her anymore. Now I must make major decisions alone. Now I must carry the responsibility of raising my three children alone. Now I must go to church and public events without her by my side. Now I must spend my vacation without her. Now I must manage my finances alone. Now I don't have her to celebrate those little victories and accomplishments that make life glorious. Now I don't have her to cheer me up when I am in a gloomy mood. Now I don't experience her love that helps correct things that I otherwise wouldn't notice alone. Now I can't enjoy her joyful and delightful presence in the house anymore. Coming home feels so much quieter—and lonely. Life has become incredibly empty without her. Ulrike has tuned my heart to play in sync with her . . . and now I am left to play a melody with half the notes. This melody is not easy to learn. Her absence has gone through me like a thread through a needle. Now everything I do is stitched with the color of her absence. Loneliness has many faces. Life is so much more enjoyable in good company. I am reminded of the ancient wisdom that "it is not good for the man to be alone" (Gen 2:18 ESV).

Intense Pain

Anyone who has not experienced the death of a spouse cannot fully fathom the pain such a separation creates for the person who is left behind. Just like there is incredible pain when new life enters the world and overwhelming joy that fills our hearts when this life is born out of love, there is raw pain when life ceases, which was connected to us through love. I felt this pain on all levels: emotionally, socially, and physically. Sadness over the loss of a loved person hurts. The emotional pain is connected to the social pain of living without her and being socially isolated. With Ulrike's death, I felt like an outsider who no longer belonged to the social group we belonged to when she was alive. Social disconnect hurts and social isolation is awkward and painful. The emotional and social disconnect and loneliness had physical reverberations. My whole body was under permanent stress. I felt tense. My body was tight. I was more irritable, edgy, and fretful. The emotional stress had physical symptoms. I did not sleep as well. I was more nervous. My immune system was weaker because of the permanent stress and worries my body was dealing with. No wonder many people get sick more easily in the initial period of grief following the loss of a loved one.

Facets and Feelings of Loss and Grief

Anxiety and Fear

Ulrike was my anchor, my safe place. Her, I could fully trust. She was my place of refuge. Her loving support gave me strength and made me feel secure. Now I can understand much better why her loss made me feel vulnerable, causing me anxiety and some fear. Losing a loved one is one of the most difficult things we ever experience in life and most people have never felt such strong emotions as they do when they experience the loss of someone they love. The strong feeling of sadness and even anger we experience over loss can be very frightening. Ulrike's death left me with erratic feelings of loneliness accompanied by a deep sense of uncertainty about my future. This is the soil which cultivates anxiety and fear.[2] Anxiety is a feeling of dread and gloomy foreboding that overcomes us in the face of uncertainty. The word anxiety comes from the Latin word *anxius*, meaning a state of agitation and distress. This distress is aggravated by the fact that the impact of loss permeates all areas of our lives in profound and unexpected ways. For me, Ulrike's loss changed the day-to-day routine of my life. I had to adjust and juggle so many logistical things. I was forced to rearrange my routines to accommodate a new family role in the absence of Ulrike. I was forced to confront my mortality in new and much more existential ways. This left me with a profound sense of insecurity. Not only did I have to learn so many new things, but I also wondered about how I would be able to cope with all this in the future by myself. This insecurity and unfamiliarity over essential aspects of life caused me to worry. I thought if she could die, anything, absolutely *anything*, could happen.

No one ever told me that grief was so closely connected to fear. In my grief, I experienced many aspects of fear. I felt afraid of more loss. I was concerned about my health and every ache or pain I felt or unfamiliar bodily signal I sensed was suspect. I was worried that another loved one could get sick and die soon. I felt afraid about my future and how I would be able to handle everything without her help. The prospect of mastering an unknown future alone was scary. In all of this, I missed Ulrike with whom I would have discussed and shared these strange feelings of insecurity and uncertainty. No wonder that a widespread reaction to the loss of a loved one is fear and anxiety. Sometimes responding to this fear, we want to appear strong. But by pretending to have everything under control

---

2. On the impact of anxiety in the process of grief see the insightful discussion in Smith, *Anxiety*. See also the helpful discussion in Tripp, *Suffering*, 57–69.

we suppress the fear and panic that lurks within us, which easily leads to even more pronounced anxiety. Mind you: anxiety creates anxiety and thus perpetuates itself.

What helped me during the first months after Ulrike's death, when feelings of anxiety and worry loomed over me and I felt like I was drowning in an endless sea of grief, was to understand the legitimacy of grief in my life and to learn to cope with it adequately. It is not wrong to be afraid, but fear should not dominate our thinking or inspire our actions. What helped me to deal with those fears was deliberately learning to trust the promises of Scripture. I learned to develop and practice an attitude of gratitude that helped me to rediscover a perspective of reality that was diminished when my anxiety grew. More about that in a later chapter on gratitude.[3] For now, let me just say that on this side of eternity no person lives a completely fear-free life. Fear can even be a good thing when we face danger. But a fearful spirit makes a cruel god and decisions based on fear tend to be decisions we later regret. When fear rules our hearts, we don't see or think about life accurately. Only with the eyes of faith can we see things that are hidden through the lens of fear. Fear is a legitimate reaction to scary things, but courage is always a personal decision! Let's remember that no matter how intense and great fear appears, it is only temporary. God's loving and tender care, however, is eternal and *will* never fade away. While there is dragon-like evil on this planet that easily scares us to the bones, this dragon can be confronted and overcome, and I had to learn to decide with God's help to face the future with courage.

Anger

Anger is a common response when we are confronted with death and loss. I certainly had moments of acute anger. Anger is a way of expressing frustration. There is nothing quite so frustrating as feeling out of control. Not being able to change things anymore made me angry. It is not surprising that anger is often a close ally to grief. I felt bouts of anger about all kinds of things: anger with myself, that I had not been with Ulrike when she died.[4]

---

3. See pp. [X-REF] on gratitude.

4. Only years later I realized in a conversation with a person who had some psychological training that I was not alone in my experience, and that many people who are in the process of dying often breathe their last breath at the very moment when the people who are closest to them have left the room. Many people are only able to leave life if no

Anger with the medical professionals who had given us a wrong diagnosis at the beginning of her hospitalization. Anger with the doctor who gave me her opinion regarding Ulrike's situation, which led me to believe that she would not die minutes after I left. I distinctly remember how feelings of anger swelled up in me when I received the news that she had died. There are things in life that you cannot change. Things you can only carry and must accept. Despite all the pain I felt I am thankful that I could realize over time how fortunate I can be for a marriage friendship in which we treated each other with love and respect and granted each other the freedom we needed to be who we are. We could approach smaller conflicts fairly soon without inflicting emotional injuries on each other and could extend forgiveness to the other if one of us failed.

Anger does not change anything. Anger does not improve the situation. Anger only makes things worse for you and for those who are confronted with your anger. What helped me in the immediate pain of this agonizing moment was a rational decision and my trust in God. While silently talking with God I still remember that I literally said to myself: Frank, this cannot be changed. Don't waste your energy over something that you have no control over. It is what it is. It was not your fault, although I felt guilty for not having been at her side. Sharing my honest feelings with God helped me to let go of these feelings and not to spend too much time worrying about them.

Sometimes we have to make rational decisions, even though we don't feel like it. It can help us to focus on what is essential for survival in a crisis. Making that rational decision and even praying about it did not fully eliminate my feelings of anger. Although praying gave me inner peace, I still faced intense feelings of pain and grief. Sometimes some of our most difficult questions are not solved by mulling over them in our minds. Sometimes new windows of understanding only open in rather unexpected situations. New perspectives and insights often come from surprising angles as we continue to navigate through uncharted territories of our life. This is a faith learning experience where we need to learn to live with the unfamiliar. Focusing on the things that need to be done now helped me to move forward and to commit my anger to God. I learned he understands my feelings, no matter how contradictory and confusing they might be. He cares. He is at our side and God can open doors for us that seem firmly

---

person is around who was closest to them. This helped me relate to my disappointment and anger differently and with a certain appreciation of what happened.

closed. God can widen the horizon of our understanding in unique ways taking us beyond the limitations of our self-made answers.

Disorientation

Without Ulrike at my side, I felt disoriented. Things we had done together, I now had to do alone. Finding my new role and place in all of this was perplexing. This perplexity and disorientation are often revealed in the apparently little things of life. For example: I emptied the dishwasher and it dawned on me that I will always have to wash the dishes by myself. I attempted to cook a meal, and I am reminded that this was her specialty, something she excelled and delighted in. Now I must do it myself—and I am not nearly as skilled as she was.

I asked myself: What is my new role in life? What is required of me? The big decisions of life, like buying new furniture or a new car, or the decision where to go on vacation, are no longer something we can discuss together. I must make these decisions alone. This leaves me perplexed and disoriented. Her absence makes me feel insecure. I miss the support, input, and wisdom of my partner for life. I miss praying with her. The existential disorientation that springs from my being alone is sobering. The thought that I have to redefine my identity as a widower made me sad. Knowing that I would never again enjoy the pleasure of being in her presence and that I would not receive those little gestures of kindness and love that she delighted to share with me added to that feeling.

Uncertainty and Insecurity

Feelings of uncertainty and insecurity crossed my mind especially when I thought about my future. Envisioning my future alone, thinking of everything I had to master without Ulrike was scary. It made me tremble. Shortly after her death I could not think too far into the future. During the early moments of my grief, I did not have the strength to even contemplate the next couple of months or years without Ulrike. It was simply too much for me. How could I bear it and manage alone? In such moments I reminded myself that I did not have to always be on top of things. I did not have to have everything planned with regard to my future. All I needed to do was to manage the next week, and often only the next day was all I could deal with. Sometimes it felt like I just had enough strength for the next hour. But in times of crisis, sometimes you only need to survive the next hour or the day ahead of you. As Jesus so aptly said: "Do not worry about tomorrow; for tomorrow will care for itself. Each day has enough trouble of its own" (Matt 6:34 NASB).

Meaninglessness

Until you have actually lost someone close to you, there is no way to fully comprehend the enormity of such an experience. Grieving the loss of a loved person raises many questions. Before Ulrike died, I enjoyed living. I was content with my life and mostly happy. I was especially happy when we were together. Without her, I repeatedly wondered about the meaning of my life. Without her, life had lost its beauty. Without her life did not make sense anymore. A few times I wondered whether life was still worth living. These destructive thoughts did not constantly occupy my thinking. But they were there, and occasionally popped up. Such thoughts are to be expected when you lose a person with whom you intimately shared your life. If those thoughts begin to dominate your thinking, seek the help of professional counselors or grief therapists.

Something that became a game changer for me and that opened my eyes to a reality beyond my immediate feelings of grief and despair was a little note that one of my students wrote to me several days after the funeral. She wrote: "I wanted to tell you something. I don't know if this helps, but I think it is important that you know this. In case there might be moments in the future, when you get so discouraged that you wish you would no longer exist in this world, you should know: You are very important to this world! Many people have been blessed through you—and will continue to be blessed through you. Please continue to live!" This thought, "Please continue to live," has encouraged me not to give up and has motivated me to continue to live. In moments of intense grief, it is easy to focus predominantly on our pain. This reminded me that I also needed to think about my sons. The encouragement of my parents, my parents-in-law, and a few other good friends who let me know that they were proud of me and prayed for me has encouraged me and helped me to continue and not give up on my journey without Ulrike.

Chapter 7

Learning to Talk about Death and Grief

TALKING ABOUT DEATH AND grief is daunting. We are often afraid to deal with it openly and our Western culture has not mastered the art of processing loss. Many are embarrassed when confronted with death because it is such a sad experience. We feel awkward. It isn't easy to mourn publicly. It leaves us feeling exposed and vulnerable. Grieving the loss of a close person can be unruly and complicated. Nicholas Wolterstorff has described the demonic character of death well when he writes: "Death is shalom's mortal enemy."[1] We don't like to talk about the threat of this enemy and the fragility of all life. Instead, we often conveniently ignore how quickly things can change from one moment to the next. The truth is, we all experience loss in life, and we all certainly will die, sooner or later. No one is exempt from death. Death is no respecter of persons. In this sense death is the great leveler and equalizer. Death does not care who you are or what your social standing is. If we can face this fact more openly and prudently, I believe we can approach it with greater courage and can support each other better as we face our mortality together and deal with it in healing ways.

It seems that in our progressive and protected Western society we sometimes forget that loss of life and loss of things is part of our human experience. No matter how much progress we have made in science and medicine, we are still exposed to death and suffering. Tragic events are a

---

1. Wolterstorff, *Lament*, 63.

reality that many would like to avoid, but we have to learn that they are nevertheless part of all human life. Paul Gerhardt, the famous Lutheran theologian and hymn writer, lived during the Thirty Years' War (1618–48), that raged between Protestants and Catholics and left much of central Europe devastated and in ruins. He lost his father when he was just twelve years old and, two years later, he lost his mother. He lost four of his five children prematurely. On top of that, he had to mourn the death of his wife, who left him a widower with his six-year-old son.[2] It amazes me time and again, how in this devastating context he was able to write some of the most beautiful and meaningful Christian hymns that are appreciated by many around the world to this day.[3] Here are a few expressive stanzas from two of his hymns that express his faith and hope in difficult times so beautifully:

> Commit thou all your griefs
> and ways into his hands;
> to his sure truth and tender care,
> who earth and heav'n commands.
> Who points the clouds their course,
> whom winds and seas obey,
> he shall direct your wand'ring feet,
> He shall prepare your way.
>   Still heavy is your heart?
> Still sink your spirits down?
> Cast off the weight, let fear depart,
> and every care be gone.
> He everywhere has sway
> and all things serve his might;
> his every act pure blessing is,
> his path unsullied light.[4]

---

2. Paul Gerhardt also experienced the devastating effects of the plague (the black death, as it was called) in 1636–37, that decimated large segments of the population in central Europe. He also witnessed the death of his brother and the almost entire destruction of his hometown through Swedish soldiers in the raging religious war.

3. Even today, and in much fewer threatening circumstances, the text and melodies of Paul Gerhardt's hymns exert an amazing influence on those who sing them and are attracted by the beauty and expressive depth of their words. Next to Martin Luther, Paul Gerhardt (1607–76) ranks as the greatest hymn writer of the Lutheran Church. On the widespread hymns of Paul Gerhardt see Dallmann, *Paul Gerhardt*, 65–69.

4. The first and third stanzas of Gerhardt, "Commit Thou All That Grieves Thee" (1653), translated by John Wesley (1737).

Learning to Talk about Death and Grief

> In Him is comfort, light and grace,
> And changeless love beyond our thought;
> The sorest pang, the worst disgrace,
> If He is there, shall harm thee not.
> He can lift off thy cross, and loose thy bands,
> And calm thy fears, nay, death is in His hands.
> Be thou content.
>
>   Thy heart's unspoken pain He knows,
> Thy secret signs He hears full well,
> What to none else thou dar'st disclose,
> To Him thou mayst with boldness tell;
> He is not far away, but ever nigh,
> And answereth willingly the poor man's cry.
> Be thou content.[5]

It seems that death and suffering were omnipresent during this period of history and people were well acquainted with the dreadful reality of death. Perhaps we enlightened citizens of the Western world, living in the twenty-first century, have pushed aside the fact that suffering, pain, sickness, and the fragility of life still exist and confront us in many unpleasant ways. We think we have mastered how to manage the incalculable intricacies of life. We boast about our scientific accomplishments. At the same time, it seems we have developed an unhealthy relationship with death and dying. We try to avoid confronting it. We want to remain forever young and, in this pursuit, have forgotten to speak adequately about the reality of death that confronts all of us. The psalm writer aptly said: "Teach us to realize the brevity of life, so that we may grow in wisdom" (Ps 90:12 NLT). I think as Christians we not only have to illustrate what it means to live a God-pleasing life by faith, but we also need to learn to face death with the resilience of faith. How we relate to death and dying should indicate to others that death is not the last horizon for us. As Christians, we have a hope that resonates in us, a hope that goes beyond the grave. The Bible tells us that there will be a resurrection when Jesus will come again in glory and will give us eternal life (2 Thess 4:13–18; 1 Cor 15:42, 54–57).

Life *is* short and often life is not fair. So, how do we articulate such injustice and the dark clouds of pain that engulf us when we grieve the loss of a person we dearly love? Echoing the words of Shakespeare's King Lear I would say: "The weight of this sad time we must obey; speak what we feel,

---

5. The second and third stanzas of Gerhardt, "Be Thou Content; Be Still Before" (1670), translated by Catherine Winkworth (1855).

not what we ought to say."[6] It is possible to talk about death and suffering in an abstract and theoretical manner. We can even use pious jargon when talking about death and dying, echoing what we think we ought to say. But when we are personally affected our perspective changes drastically.

The Lost Art of Lament

I have noticed, especially among confessing Christians, that many find it difficult to express their true feelings when facing tragedy, suffering, and loss. Instead, many say what they think Christians ought to say in the face of adversity. The discrepancy between the pain they feel over the loss of a dear person and the way they piously talk about it may lead to even greater problems. It can negatively affect our spiritual perception and even hinder a healing process in dealing with loss in life. Also, it frequently brings into question our authenticity in how we deal with the terror of death and bad things that happen to us.

I am convinced we need to rediscover the grace and blessing of the biblical art of lament. In dealing with suffering, injustice, and the pain of death "lament invites us to grieve and trust, to struggle and believe."[7] Rather than ignoring the evil we face or denying the pain we experience by sugarcoating it with pious phrases or by pretending we are okay—when we are really not okay—we have to learn to live with unanswerable questions that every case of suffering poses. We need to recover how to honestly express what we experience and how to bring our sorrow and open questions to God.

Lament is a statement of faith in which we cry in our suffering and honestly wrestle with the paradox of the reality of pain and the promise of God's goodness. Lament is only possible if we believe in God's mercy, goodness, and grace. It is rooted in the hope that God will deliver and in the conviction that God is almighty and good. Without the belief in a good and loving God, who is also sovereign and omnipotent, there would be no lament! Lament helps us deal with the reality of a hard and unfair life while trusting in God's love and sovereignty. Lament is how we as committed Christians bring our sorrow to God. It processes our pain. Without lament bitterness and anger will dampen our spiritual life and even kill it. Lament helped me to acknowledge the injustice that is in this sinful world and the

---

6. Shakespeare, "William Shakespeare Quotes" (*King Lear*, act 5, sc. 3).
7. Vroegop, *Dark Clouds*, 20.

bad things that happen even to very good people while still declaring that suffering and pain will not have the final say. God does not ignore or avoid our pain. Instead, God invites us to be honest with ourselves and with him and to dare to lament those opaque and incomprehensible things that happen to us. God is not offended by our lament. He invites us to honestly bring even our darkest and most grievous thoughts into his presence. The psalm writers have exercised this in remarkable and even shocking ways. Lament creates a pathway between the dire situation we face now and the "not yet." It bridges the gap between hopelessness and coming hope. It acknowledges the painful reality we face now and helps us to hold on to God's goodness, even though we don't have all the answers or do not understand every why.[8] Lament is a godly concept, a biblical way of prayer, and a powerful spiritual exercise in our season of sorrow.[9] In lament, we stop pretending. In lament, we acknowledge we are no longer in control of our situation. In lament, we honestly pour out our hearts to God. Lament is a way to express our pain. Lament is a reaction to the absence of God's shalom.[10]

In my own journey with grief, and in my conversation with others, I noticed that often the biggest obstacle to lament is that people are unsure if it is acceptable to express those feelings to God. We are accustomed to the words of the apostle Paul that we should "rejoice in the Lord always" (Phil 4:4 ESV). How do we follow this command and simultaneously lament? How do we—when experiencing our pain and suffering—praise God and lament without offending him? The example of numerous biblical writers and heroes of faith tells us that lament is not wrong. In fact, it is essential to deal with pain and suffering in healing ways. However, true lament can only happen in the context of a safe and loving relationship, where I fully trust God and have the freedom to be my truest self, without any fear that God will walk away from me or stop loving me. Claus Westermann, a famous Old Testament theologian, has aptly pointed out that in the Bible lament is at the heart of the relationship between God and his people.[11] According to Westermann "it is an illusion to suppose or postulate that there could be a relationship with God in which there was only praise and never

---

8. At least one-third of the 150 psalms are laments. This makes lament the largest category in the entire Psalter (Waltke et al., *Psalms*, 1). One entire book of the Bible, the book of Lamentations, is devoted to lament.

9. Sampson, *Louder Song*, 13.

10. Sampson, *Louder Song*, 27.

11. Westermann, "Role of Lament," 20–21.

lamentation. Just as joy and sorrow in alternation are part of the human existence (Gen 2–3), so praise and lamentation are part of [our] relationship to God."[12] As Christians, we lament because evil things are part of our lives. We lament because God invites us to bring our lament to him. In fact, God has given us the language of lament. The God of the Bible is a personal God who is fully worthy of our praise and worship, but he is also worthy to hear about our suffering and sadness in our lament. "If we never acknowledge our pain to God, we will never truly know what it means to praise him on the other side of suffering. It is in our honest crying out *to God* about our pain that our worship *of God* grows more authentic."[13] This makes our walk with God real and is an expression of a deepening relationship with him.

Lament does not bring immediate comfort or resolution to the tension we face. Lament is not a silver bullet. Grief is a ferocious tiger. But lament honestly and specifically names a situation or circumstance that is painful, wrong, or unjust and does not align with God's character and thus opens the door to healing by giving our pain a name. It is a passionate prayer in pain that leads to trust.[14] It reminds our hearts and minds that we believe God is truly good and that we experience a tension between the character of God and the painful circumstances we are in. While lament starts with the things we don't understand, it does not end with complaining. Lament is not wallowing in our complaints. Lament is not complaining as an end in and of itself.[15] As we surrender our pain to God, he shifts our focus toward himself. Our hope in suffering is not a self-fabricated solution. It is not something that grows out of us. In lament, our last word is about the object of our hope, the very one all laments long for and lead us to: Jesus, who through his suffering and death on the cross has saved us. In him, all the promises of God find their Yes! (2 Cor 1:20).

The promises in the Bible gave me a glimmer of hope. Initially, I could not imagine how the truth of Jesus' words "My peace I give to you" (John 14:27 ESV) could come true. I remember visiting my aunt Hilde and her new husband with my sons several months after Ulrike died. Both had lost their spouses several years previously and were now happily married. Talking with them about my intense feelings of loss, even many months after

---

12. Westermann, "Role of Lament," 27.

13. Sampson, *Louder Song*, 26.

14. This has been pointed out by Vroegop, *Dark Clouds*, 28, in his excellent book on lament.

15. Vroegop, *Dark Clouds*, 45, 53, 68.

Learning to Talk about Death and Grief

Ulrike's death, I said that I didn't have the impression that this would ever get any better. Harold kindly and gently said: "I know the feeling! This is how any normal person feels after dealing with a significant loss in life. But believe me," he continued, "the pain grows milder over time. The rawness of the open wound will slowly heal, even if you don't feel like it right now." His words proved true in my experience. In Matt 5 we read: "Blessed are those who mourn for they will be comforted" (Matt 5:4 ESV). In every loss, God remains the God of comfort. No matter whether it is the painful loss that comes with the death of someone we love, or anything else that leaves us crushed and discouraged, God remains a God of comfort (2 Cor 1:3) and is ready to restore shalom in our hearts and minds. The promises in his word were an anchor of hope in my mourning. To know that Jesus experienced the pain of separation through death himself. This makes him a savior who is not aloof but who fully understands and therefore could send me the very help I truly needed (Heb 4:14–16).

I also experienced comfort and encouragement in the company of trusted friends. When I shared some of the complexities of my loss with others it made things easier. However, for that to happen, I had to be willing to be vulnerable in sharing some of my life. After Ulrike's death, I repeatedly invited my parents-in-law to come for a couple of days to help us with things around the house and keep my sons and me company. As they were retired, they had the flexibility to do this and lovingly helped us in unobtrusive ways. My mother-in-law prepared delicious and healthy food that we enjoyed. They helped to keep our apartment clean and cozy. They did some of the grocery shopping, or they just were there with me, with us, talking, when we needed someone to talk to, being quiet when we were not in the mood to talk, and often just listening attentively. They intuitively provided some structure and continuity to our daily routine. In the late afternoon, we would often enjoy a delightful teatime with some homemade cookies. I would share with them the letters of condolences I had received. We would talk about those passages that were written with understanding and that provided comfort because they recounted personal incidences with Ulrike. It provided an opportunity for all of us to grieve and be comforted at the same time. We were suffering and healing together.

I experienced the greatest peace in those private moments when I opened up to God, telling him honestly about my fears and longings, lamenting the things I did not understand. I talked with God as I would talk to my best friend. I call it praying. It is not the kind of prayer where I just spoke to God about what I wished to have, what I wanted to receive, and what I thought he needed to give me. The prayers with God that refreshed me the most were honest conversations with God where God became central. In those prayers, I did not thoughtlessly repeat certain prayer phrases. Instead, my focus was on him as a trusted friend, because I had experienced him not just as my redeemer and Lord, but as a faithful friend, in whose companionship I was flourishing. To be with him, just for the pleasure of being in his presence, was important to me. It was invigorating. It gave me new strength. In his presence, I felt sheltered.[16] When I recommitted my life and my fears to his good and tender care peace entered my heart. It calmed me down. This happened often when I was driving in my car, especially on those long-distance trips when I was alone in my car for several hours and had time to listen to the words of beautiful Christian music. Listening to music from John Rutter, or time-proven hymns and some modern songs from Fernando Ortega and other gifted musicians, was a great blessing. While alone in the car I would sing along. Nobody could hear my croaky voice. Quite often I found myself starting to cry because the lyrics and the melodies touched my heart. I was reminded that others before me had experienced their share of pain and suffering that led to the composition of some of this beautiful and expressive music. I also realized that it is extremely difficult to sing a hopeful song aloud and retain negative sentiments and feel depressed. Good music is a mood changer and has proven to be a faithful companion in the process of lament over the years.

    My lament also encompassed a loss that became obvious only over time. The longer the time distance grew between us the more I noticed that there were moments I had shared with Ulrike, aspects of her personality, that I could not remember clearly anymore. Some of the photographs of our family reminded me of incidents that my mind was slowly forgetting. My sons recounted anecdotes that I could not recall. This created a different sadness. The further I moved away from Ulrike, with the passage of time, the more I mourned the things that I slowly forgot. The sound of her voice (there are very few audio recordings of her voice), the scent of her smell with the fragrance of her favorite perfume, many of the things she said and did. Grief is complex. It is not easily explained or handled. These secondary losses emerged only over time. They also are a consequence of her death. Because they emerge only later does not make them less impactful

---

16. I have described this kind of prayer in the chapter "Prayer That Is Pleasing to God" in Hasel, *Longing for God*, 42–45.

or less difficult to handle. For me, a particularly helpful way of dealing with the challenge of forgetfulness is to commit my thoughts and memories to writing.

The Power of Writing

Dealing with loss is complicated. Coping with the reality of grief within us is not much easier. In my journey with loss and grief, I found it helpful to write down my thoughts, my feelings, and my lament. Expressing what was swirling around in my mind in handwritten words, on actual paper, was a healing process. It opened the path for a restorative journey in my grief and gave structure to my memory. Such a writing process is a journey into memory and cleared my mind. The act of physically sitting down and taking a pen to pin down and express my thoughts or to put them in order with the help of a keyboard was an important exercise that helped me process my grief and to relate to it in healing ways. It also alleviated some of my anxiety. Writing out my grief, memories, and feelings I connect with the loss of Ulrike has become a powerful tool for me not only to remember her, but it also helped to restore my sanity.

Writing is very different from thinking or talking. Something happens to you when you write that does not happen when you just think about it. Writing has a way of structuring your thoughts and moving your thinking forward. There is a deeper intention behind what we write that has a positive impact on our brain and our whole being. It clarifies the conflicting and bewildering thoughts we carry in our minds. It helps to let out what we hide inside our heads. Writing about grief has been popular for a long time. From C. S. Lewis's classic book *A Grief Observed*[17] to Nicholas Wolterstorff's moving book *Lament for a Son*,[18] writers and readers alike have been drawn to stories of loss. It is not just that the writers of these stories experience catharsis in writing while sharing their stories, but often the readers are blessed as well.

I started writing about my feelings during a three-week health retreat to recuperate from the stress and physical impact I suffered following the death of Ulrike. In writing down what had happened to me and how I felt about it, I was able to reflect on my experience and gain a new perspective. It not only helped to sort many of my thoughts, it was literally a relief. It

17. Lewis, *Grief Observed*.
18. Wolterstorff, *Lament*.

set me free to look at life with new eyes. It was the beginning of journaling some of my thoughts and impressions. A book grew out of this experience that helped me live through all my small and big challenges with courage.[19] It also helped me remember the small and large blessings I encountered along the journey.

You don't need to be an experienced writer or bring years of journaling experience to this task. There are different ways of using writing to help you reflect on your experience. You can write a letter to the person who is dead. You can start journaling regularly. You can write down things that are worth remembering. As you try to find the form of writing that is helpful for you, remember: don't expect to be an accomplished writer right away. You don't need to. Don't expect to write beautiful prose that will undo this terrible thing that has happened to you. Simply write your thoughts, and your story. "Good writing is about telling the truth."[20] It can be the beginning of building a bridge that helps you to remember what connects you with the person you love and shows who you were and who you have become. It is a wonderful antidote against forgetfulness. Remember, no one must read what you write. If you don't know how to start and what to write, here are a few ideas that may help get you started:

- Write about one of your favorite memories together
- Write about something you lost and will never get back
- Write about the things that scare you
- Write about a time when you knew you had done the right thing
- Write about some of the things that have happened since they died
- Write about something you feel guilty or sorry about that you wish to apologize for
- Write about what you remember when . . .
- Write about what you loved when you . . .
- Write what your/their favorite clothing, smell, song, holiday, food was

19. Hasel, *Longing for God*. I found the encounter with God in the Bible and in prayer life changing. The spiritual impulses described in this book have helped me to open new horizons for my own walk with God and have helped me stay spiritually sane and even joyful in the middle of the pain and grief I suffered.

20. Lamott, *Bird by Bird*, 3. As Anne Lamott has succinctly stated: "We are a species that needs and wants to understand who we are. Sheep lice do not seem to share this longing, which is one reason they write so very little" (*Bird by Bird*, 3).

- Write thoughts of thankfulness for all the ways they have enriched your life and made you feel loved and supported
- Write what they have taught you

These are just a few suggestions. Feel free to enlarge this list with your thoughts and reflections. There is no perfect time to start this work. But it is never too late to begin writing. I hope you feel encouraged to start writing down what is on your mind. Don't be scared. Let your thoughts and emotions flow unto the page.

Calling Death by Its Name

I noticed that in conversations about death we often avoid expressing the inevitable reality of death by using its name. Perhaps it is too painful to say it out loud. Perhaps we are afraid to call the greatest enemy of life by name. Instead, we resort to descriptions of impending death: "she will not live much longer"; "she will not be with us anymore"; "she will be gone soon"; etc. I later noticed in my grieving process that it took quite a while for me to verbalize the words: "She died!" "She is dead!" At first, I was not able to express it directly. It was too painful for me to say it. Having the courage to call death by its cold name is the beginning of a healing process. When you look the unpleasant reality of death in its face and do not slip into euphemisms to avoid its harsh reality, healing begins. Healing takes time. Don't feel pressured to rush things. As Christians, we know that death is not our final destination. Beyond the grave, there is the hope of a life without pain, sorrow, and tears. There is the promise of a new heaven and a new earth in which God will wipe away every tear from our eyes. There will be no more mourning, or crying, or pain, and there will no longer be any death, we are told in Rev 22:3–5. Then death is overcome by love and all those who have put their trust in Jesus will share in the resurrection of the risen Christ. This knowledge about this beautiful spiritual reality does not eliminate the pain death causes now. On occasions, some Christians pretend the agony of loss and grief is not so acute for them, as if the knowledge of the resurrection is the panacea for all the pain that death brings. I firmly believe in the truthfulness of the biblical teaching of the resurrection to eternal life of all those who have put their faith in Jesus Christ alone. I certainly look forward to the joy of meeting Ulrike again on the resurrection morning. But that belief does not eliminate the pain of our separation. It is not the cure for all my sorrow and grief. This side of heaven, death does something to all of us that changes our lives in many significant and important ways.

Chapter 8

Death's Impact: A World Turned Inside Out

WHEN ULRIKE DIED, LIFE as I knew it ended. My life changed in an instant. It altered my existence and changed me in significant ways. While everyone's experience will vary, certain aspects seem to be universally present when we encounter the loss of a person we love and with whom we closely shared our lives. What follows are some of those feelings and realities from my perspective.

It Forced Me to Learn to Live Alone

This is obvious, but it needs to be mentioned. Just as I had to adjust to living together with Ulrike when we got married, I now had to learn to live without her. This is an ongoing process of unlearning and relearning. After we got married, learning to live together with Ulrike was motivated by love and accompanied by exciting expectations and the prospect of intimately sharing our lives. Now things were reversed. I had to learn to live alone again and live well. Before we got married, I lived a happy life. Enjoying life alone—and in the company of good friends—before we got married helped me to enjoy the pleasure of her unique company in our marriage even more. She enriched my life in so many ways and in new dimensions. While my life was certainly happy with her, I was not fixated on her to make me feel happy. My life without her will never be the same, but my earlier experience as a happy bachelor helped me to slowly regain the perspective that life can have enjoyable moments—even without her! This is what I needed to discover and learn anew.

It Provoked Feelings of Envy

One emotion I felt very strongly during the early weeks and months after Ulrike's death was envy. Envy is not an enjoyable feeling. It leaves you restless and dissatisfied. It generates malicious feelings preventing you from enjoying the success and happiness of others. Ultimately envy leads us into isolation because we compare ourselves with others. When you begin to constantly ponder what others have, and you don't, it either leads you into pride, because you think that you are better than others, or it leads you into unhappiness because it creates nagging feelings of being disadvantaged. Both feelings are detrimental to our spiritual health. The feelings envy generates are intense and powerful. They are never satisfied. Jealousy and envy have disastrous effects on our quality of life. They are extremely destructive to the way we relate to each other.[1]

I remember the envy and pain I felt shortly after Ulrike had died when I saw couples walking hand in hand or hugging and kissing each other. It felt so unfair. I felt envious when I witnessed how they were enjoying life together. I felt envious when I saw them spending time together or they were able to go on a vacation together. Watching them simply enjoy each other's company was hard for me. Seeing their happiness with each other made me jealous and unhappy. Why could they still enjoy the pleasure of their friendship when I was deprived of experiencing the same with Ulrike? How unfair, I thought! The longer I entertained these nagging thoughts, the more unbearable my situation became.

Slowly I came to realize and understand that envy is a form of blindness, which prevents me from adequately and realistically seeing my gifts and the things that God has given me. Instead, my perception is narrowed to what I no longer have and focuses on the things other people have. It has been said that:

> The view of envy,
> to the dismay of all,

---

[1]. On the destructive nature of envy and some helpful perspectives to overcome it see Hasel, *Living for God*, 45–52.

Death's Impact: A World Turned Inside Out

sees all the other things as big and strong
but all my own achievements small.[2]

Envy narrows our horizon. Envy erects walls that separate us from each other and ultimately even from God. We become prisoners of our own feelings of deprivation. Strong feelings, like envy, can never be obliterated just by rational thought. They require a transformation of the heart and, I believe, the experience of divine grace. Otherwise, they will always come back to haunt and torment us. Through experiencing God's grace and better understanding the uniqueness of my situation and the value of my life I was able to let go of unhealthy envious comparisons with others. This takes time and, I believe, a change of mind that grows out of an experience of God's tender love for us. It also requires a willingness to see and acknowledge the good and lovely in others. It needs open eyes to discover and enjoy the beauty[3] that still exists in this world.

I began to see a way out of the prison of envy through some wisdom from my mother-in-law. For many years she had worked in a hospital where she supervised and accompanied people who were no longer able to live by themselves. For most, a restriction of freedom and inability to do certain things we enjoy is viewed as a severe limitation in our quality of life and often leads to unhappiness and dissatisfaction. My mother-in-law counseled those people not to focus on the things they were no longer able to do, but rather to focus on the many things they were still able to do or were able to learn to do. When confronted with adversity and loss our first reaction is to focus on the very things we lost. This is normal. Pain demands to be heard and it focuses on those things we no longer have. Focusing only on the things we don't have any more blinds us to the manifold beauty and richness of the lives that we still can enjoy. We need to regain this perspective. What helped me to appreciate this broader picture was to practice some simple but powerful steps to regain an attitude of gratitude.[4]

I also realized a simple but profound insight from the concluding sentence of the tenth commandment. Here God opens to us a new paradigm

---

2. This is my English translation of a German poem by Friedrich Rückert: "*Der Blick des Neides sieht zu seiner eignen Pein nur alles Fremde groß und alles Eigene klein*" (Rückert, *Die Weisheit*, 89).

3. On the startling presence of beauty in this world see the stimulating thoughts in Ganssle, *Our Deepest Desire*, 73–76. For inspiring thoughts on gratitude and the beauty of nature see the TED talk by Louie Schwartzberg, "Nature. Beauty. Gratitude."

4. For more detail on gratitude see 106–8.

on how we should relate to each other. God knew about the destructive influence of envy in our lives. His divine words of wisdom respond to the power of envy. After listing seven specific things that we should not covet we read the seemingly insignificant last clause: *or anything that is your neighbor's"* (Deut 5:21). Isn't that generalization a dilution of the previous specifics?

No, a Hebrew person thinks more holistically. Here in the final words of the Ten Commandments, the short Hebrew word "*kól*" is translated by the English word "anything." In Hebrew "*kól*" means "anything," but it can also denote the entirety, everything, the totality of it all. When we hear the sound of the tenth commandment with this understanding, then God wants to tell us: *You shall not covet your neighbor's wife; and you shall not covet your neighbor's house, his field, his male servant, his female servant, his ox, his donkey, or everything else, i.e., the totality of all that is your neighbor's!* (Deut 5:21).

Here we encounter how God sees us human beings. God sees us in the context of the totality of our life! We often covet this or that in the life of another person. But God sees us much more comprehensively! It is so easy to envy individual things. But the question we must face at this point is this: do you really want to have *everything* of the other person?

Not just the attractive and beautiful wife of your neighbor—but also the mother-in-law and her extended family, that goes along with her?

Not just your neighbor's big house, but also the large mortgage payments and utility bills and taxes that go along with it?

Not just the money the other person has—but also the burden of the responsibility for the money?

Not just the impressive German sports car—but also the exorbitant leasing and insurance payments to drive it?

Not just the success in another's professional career, but also the hard and enduring work that made it possible?

Not just the sweet cherries from your neighbors' garden, but also the time-consuming care for the garden and its products?

In other words, everything—i.e., the totality of it all? Do you want to trade with his or her entire *life*? Would you be willing to live in his or her skin—completely? It is this totality of life that God has in view. This is what he wants to protect. Therefore, God himself wants to safeguard what is ours. When I started to see others and myself in this totality, rather than envying only what seemed desirable in my eyes, it opened a new perspective that

Death's Impact: A World Turned Inside Out

enabled me to see the other person and myself with God's eyes. It helped me to learn that I could be happy for the things this person enjoyed and for the many things that I could still enjoy in my own life.

Often it is a long time until we realize, acknowledge, and accept(!) that part of every life is the experience of loss in some form or another. We must learn to let go of things we would love to have but don't. We must learn that we cannot have everything in life. It is important to learn to adequately deal with this painful reality of life and be able to mourn over this fact. Envy hinders this important aspect of grieving. The person who is jealous and full of envy cannot adequately deal with the things she doesn't have and becomes unable to concentrate on those things she has. Envy hinders us from enjoying what we still have. With God's help we can learn to focus on what we have, rather than what we don't have, and this enables us to find new ways to put our abilities, talents, and resources to good use.

When I realized this in my own life, I started to breathe again, spiritually speaking. I started to tell God honestly and openly the things I missed, my unfulfilled dreams, my disappointments, my deficiencies, and my inner longings. As I did this, I experienced the wonder and miracle of God's transforming grace. Slowly I was able to accept, with God's help, the situation I found myself in. I began to refocus and learned to see the many things I still had and could use for his glory. This new perspective of seeing the other person in his or her totality was a window that generated deeper joy and brought satisfaction in my own life because it enriched my relationships and enhanced the quality of my life.

It Diminished My Desire to Live

Without Ulrike, my world was emptier, and living alone was less attractive. "Should I care about anything anymore?" I was wondering at times. Sometimes I was tempted to think: No! I felt I had been robbed of the love of my life, and our future. I felt as if there was no joy or hope in the world anymore. What could the world offer me that I still wanted? The experience of significant loss easily triggers strong feelings of futility. There is a lack of purpose in the absence of the one you shared your life with.

Living alone again, after enjoying a meaningful and fulfilled marriage life, requires a lot of self-discipline. It requires determination to carry on. It started with the small things, like making my bed in the morning, getting properly and attractively dressed, taking good care of myself and my health, eating and drinking healthily and regularly, and exercising sufficiently to keep me vital and fit. For me, these daily routines were a blessing. Feeling responsible for my children also helped me. I knew they still needed me. Their existence and future gave me a purpose and provided a reason to carry on. It made me accountable. I did not want them to experience the loss of both of their parents in close succession. I wanted to be there for them. I loved them so much.

I had to carry on teaching from Monday through Friday. Often, it was a real challenge to stand in front of my students and speak. It was not easy to teach them insights from the Bible and how to live accordingly when I felt so weak and inadequate. Yet, I saw in their faces that they were looking at me to see how I would stand the real test of faith, coping with one of the most difficult things a person can encounter: the loss of your spouse. What was my faith worth, if it was not able to stand its ground authentically in a situation where it was needed the most?

I am grateful for my students during this time. They bore with me. They patiently and graciously were there, and I could tell that this was not easy for them either. Yes, there were brief grief moments where life did not seem worth living. In some of these moments, I reminded myself that my life was not yet over and that God still wanted to use me to be a blessing to others, especially my children, but also to my students and to all the people I love. There are many who wrestle with the dark shadows of similar temptations. Never underestimate the power for good that can come from a small handwritten encouragement or a text message that can lift the burden that rests upon our shoulders and make life so much more bearable. Never hesitate to actually express your honest appreciation for another person and tell her that you are glad that she exists. This might just be what she needs to hear. It often made my day.

It Created a Lack of Security

Words are inadequate to fully describe the darker feelings that accompanied the loss of my wife. After Ulrike's death, the feelings of fear can be compared to the uncertainty of entering a strange, hostile, and foreign land, that looked like a barren desert. I must travel this dangerous and rough terrain alone, with an unknown destiny, not knowing how or whether I would make it. The person who had given meaning and orientation to my life is no more. With her at my side traveling would have been less scary

Death's Impact: A World Turned Inside Out

and even an exciting adventure. Without her, I lost the refuge I experienced in her unconditional love for me. Her death robbed me of a fundamental sense of security that I experienced in her presence. Her absence was not just a minor, temporary inconvenience. It was permanent. Now I was alone. I felt threatened by all the demands and responsibilities that seem to rest on my shoulders alone. This thought was overwhelming. It made me tremble. Mind you: such feelings are normal. It is no wonder that people who have lost a loved one often are willing to get a new life insurance or other policy that would ensure greater protection and security.

One particular area where I experienced this fear acutely was the lack of security I sensed with regard to my own life, and how this could affect our children. I thought, if this had happened to Ulrike, anything, literally anything, could happen to me or to other people that I loved. I now had the sole responsibility to care for our children. I had to provide for their and my safety. They had just lost their mother. They were half-orphans. I did not want them to also lose their father. I worried about what would happen to them if something happened to me! In my work I traveled by car quite a bit, and so I was afraid that something could happen to me in a senseless car accident. I felt this even more acutely as we had, for financial reasons, always driven older, used cars, that did not have the same advanced safety features as many of the newer cars have. My fears were further aggravated by the vivid memory of the untimely death of my uncle, who had died in a tragic car accident, just a couple of days after his youngest daughter got married. I did not want my sons to lose their father through a similar accident. I wanted to be as safe and secure as possible. For me, the epitome of a safe car was a Volvo. So, I needed a Volvo to ease my fears and anxiety. I reasoned, if I drove a Volvo, I, and my sons, would be safe. I could not afford to buy a new Volvo, but with the little savings I had, I was able to buy a used Volvo V70 station wagon. My dream car! I guess God must have smiled at my desperate and fearfully limited thinking. Getting the Volvo to guarantee my safety taught me an important lesson. The Volvo was a great car. It drove well. It was very safe. But just a couple months later there were some major problems with the engine that put me at risk. The problem could not be solved for quite a while and eventually would cost me a fortune in repairs. Driving this "safe" car completely depleted all my financial savings and made me realize that my safety was not found in a certain car. Ultimately it is in the hands of God, who sees me, knows all my needs, and takes good care of me. No safety feature is so secure as to protect me from all harm. Only God can provide the safety I need. Only God can drive out any fear that might lurk in my heart. Later in life, I would experience this repeatedly in different circumstances when I transitioned to a new professional environment and moved to a different country where I had no family and friends close by.

It Raised a Relational Riddle

As time passed, perhaps the question I was asked most frequently was whether I was still single. This question comes with typical bureaucratic regularity from the German pension authority. Because Ulrike worked as a teacher in a public school in Germany I am entitled to a very small pension, as long as I do not remarry. If I do, I will forfeit my entitlement to my widower's pension. While these bureaucratic inquiries are sometimes a nuisance, I understand their necessity.

What I didn't need or like, however, were the well-intentioned and sometimes nosy comments regarding whether I had remarried or planned to get married again. People would say, "You are still young and handsome," "There are plenty of suitable women," and some would even make specific recommendations or try their hand at matchmaking. I got the distinct impression that, in their mind, I needed to remarry and then everything would be good again and they would not have to worry about me. These situations were often awkward. I felt uneasy and I definitely did not feel understood. I felt that, in their eyes, if I did not remarry, then something must be wrong with me. It seemed to me, that they were not interested in how I really felt or what I thought was good for me. Rather, they wanted to help me so that *they* would not have to worry about me anymore.

Of course, I thought of getting remarried; who wouldn't? It is a legitimate and good option. Every person is different and has different needs and longings. When you are married to someone with whom you share a lot of things in common and are loving and supportive of each other, it can be a little bit like heaven on earth. If you marry for the sake of being married and do not want to be alone, the reverse is true.

To remarry after the death of a spouse is not as easy as it looks. It is wonderful to be married. But it is not wrong to stay single! Perhaps what we need to learn more than anything else is to live life to the glory of God, whether we are married or widowed or single. Whether I am married or widowed I need to learn to trust God more fully and live a life that is grounded in faith and sustained by God's grace. The Bible tells us that God's grace is fully sufficient for us, no matter whether we are married or not! (2 Cor 12:9).

It Changed Thought Patterns

Experiencing death and grief was an emotional alchemy that impacted and blurred my thinking. Grief has definite effects on our ability to concentrate, make decisions, find things, or simply think clearly. These cognitive effects are sometimes referred to as "grief fog" because you feel as if everything around you is shrouded in a thick fog.

The pain of grief kidnapped my thoughts. In so doing it had a powerful effect on my emotions and the way I thought. It produced a new awareness of things I had never had before. Suffering and grief tended to direct my focus on myself. My mind was assaulted with so many new things that needed to be considered, that needed to be faced, and that needed to be decided. Fears began to swallow me up. I started wondering how I would ever be able to cope. I realized that fear often made me lose sight of the most basic and obvious things. I easily forgot things that guided me in the past. I needed to remind myself of what motivated me in the past and what was my source of comfort in the present. For my survival, it was crucial to know and to remind myself where to look for my security and hope. For me, God's tender love had always been a source of strength and comfort. Bible passages that reminded me of God's love and care became my favorites.

When we are confronted with hardship and suffering it is easy to question God's goodness and power, and many have concluded that God does not exist or, if he does, that he does not care. For me, it is crystal clear that God is good. From God's word I know that there is no shadow or turning in him (Jas 1:17). He is not responsible for the existence of evil. He *is* love (1 John 4:8, 16) and he does not delight in the death of others, not even of the wicked (Ezek 33:11). For him death is an enemy (1 Cor 15:26). God has demonstrated his power over death through the resurrection of Jesus. God himself is affected by evil and death and feels with us because he knows what it meant to see his one and only Son die on the cross. Therefore, he is able to intercede for us and provide the very help that we need in our difficulties (Heb 4:15). God does not delight in suffering and death. He is not the source of our affliction. God has given us unmistakable proof of his love for us in sending his Son Jesus. He wants to save us, not destroy us.

He takes no pleasure in our suffering. God rather suffers with us. On the other hand, Satan delights in everything evil. Satan is happy when we are in pain. He has won his case when he succeeds in shipwrecking our faith and undermining our trust in God. Satan enjoys when we begin to doubt God's goodness and mercy. The Bible tells us that Satan is the great *diabolos*, who jumbles everything up (John 8:48). He creates a false picture of God and leads us to mistrust him and his goodness. Ulrike and I did not want to give Satan the pleasure of succeeding in this seduction. What is happening on this earth is an example to the whole universe.[5]

Without the clear word of God, the pain of the separation from Ulrike would have been swallowed up in the tyranny of fear when pondering the problems suffering poses. It required intentional rethinking and deliberately refocusing my attention to break free from the grip of fear and from false concepts of God.

It Raises Questions about God and the Here and Now

Suffering always puts our spiritual life under attack. In my grief, I realized I was susceptible to temptations that otherwise would not affect me. Suffering grief pushed me to the borders of my faith. I began to think things I had never thought before, questioning things that I had assumed were firmly settled in my mind and heart. It challenged old assumptions and replaced them with questions that were difficult to find satisfying answers to. It made me spiritually vulnerable where I thought I was strong. I was tempted to seek answers where God was silent. Such existential questions are exhausting spiritually and physically taxing. They even have the potential to shipwreck our faith (1 Tim 1:19).

Suffering, pain, and grief might raise some theoretical questions, but their experience is never abstract, theoretical, or impersonal. They are real, tangible, personal, and specific. Suffering has deeply personal, theological, and profoundly spiritual connotations.[6] It has the power to expose the true basis of your trust. It also can teach us that we are not in control of everything in our lives and thus provides an opportunity to learn to trust God more fully.

---

5. If you would like to explore this complex subject in greater depth from a biblical and theological perspective I recommend the book by Peckham, *Theodicy of Love*.

6. On this crucial issue see the helpful insights in Tripp, *Suffering*.

Death's Impact: A World Turned Inside Out

I found it very comforting to know that the God of the Bible never looks down on a sufferer. He never mocks my pain, never condemns me in my struggle. God hears my cries. He is personally affected by my pain. He understands my sorrow. He knows what it means to see his only Son die.

It Catapulted Me into a New Social Category

Life is constantly changing. Some changes are subtle and evolve slowly. When your life partner dies the change is seismic. I have dealt with the death of my grandparents and parents. I have experienced the death of my dear uncle and a beloved aunt. I have seen some of my students and colleagues die. But the death of my wife did something to me that no other death accomplished. It initiated a significant change that I did not recognize and understand for quite some time. Several months after Ulrike's death a good friend alerted me to this new reality. The death of your spouse changes your social identity. It affects your standing in society. The moment you get married you are no longer a bachelor, you are no longer single, you now belong to the category "married." This is recognized by society and the law. It affects the way you interact with other people. It has legal implications. It changes some of your friendships. When you become a widower or widow the reverse happens. Your social standing changes again. I realized immediately: I no longer belonged to those who were married! I had moved to a different social category. I was single again, albeit in a very different way than before I got married. Society conveys this new form of existence with a label, reflecting this new social standing: a person who has lost his or her spouse now is called a widower or a widow. No other death makes you a widower or a widow. No other death has such drastic implications for your social life and your existence.

When you are widowed, this social shift brings with it a distinct loss of identity. Who am I now? Repeatedly I found myself wondering: *Am* I still married to Ulrike (that is how I felt) or *was* I married to her? Has my relationship with and my affection for her changed with her death? Is she still my wife or is she no longer my wife? Who am I without her? Am I single now? Is a widower a single person? Of course, he is, but at the same time, he is much more than a single person who has never been married. After all, the official designation is widower, not single. So, what is my role in society, in the church, and in my family? I noticed that losing my marriage partner also brought with it a certain (although not complete) shift in my circle of friends. Being a widower rearranged the combinations of people with whom I socialized and resonated. Sometimes I found myself drawn into a closer connection with people who were almost strangers, but whose experiences echoed my own and created a bond of understanding.

Chapter 9

Myths of Closure

Reoccurring Grief

GRIEF IS WEIRD. It doesn't stop because you move on with your life. It just follows you. Grief is not something we ever leave behind! Grief is a companion who stays. When you lose a person you love deeply the intervals between various grief responses and grief reactions lengthen over time. But grief never disappears. It always hovers at the edge of our awareness, prepared to surface at any time and often in the least expected ways. This might sound rather depressing, but before you get too depressed over the permanent prospect of grief it is necessary to understand two important things: (a) grief often coexists with other delightful feelings, such as joy and happiness; and, even more importantly, (b) grief is an expression of our love for the person who is no longer here in person. Allow me to unpack these aspects a bit more. Let's begin with the coexistence of joy and grief.

Grief and Happiness Can Coexist

Often joy and grief occur simultaneously. Moments of great joy are often also coupled with intense feelings of grief because the person with whom we want to share our joy and happiness is no longer with us. Sometimes when I have enjoyed some beautiful music, a masterful piece of art, the grandeur of the ocean and majestic mountains, the happiness of young children playing peacefully, the pleasure of a well written book, or the culinary delight of a new recipe I sadly realize that we cannot enjoy them together. The experience of joy and grief are often closely allied. Sometimes we compartmentalize joy and grief as if they exist on opposite sides. We try to move people from the sadness of grief to the delightful and happy part of life. We want to leave grief behind. We want to move on without it. This is particularly true for people who are trying to help those who grieve. But anyone who has experienced grief knows too well that this is not how life works. Grief does not disappear suddenly or evaporate over time. Grief is intricately connected to so many facets of life that it is an integral part of who we are. We would have to eliminate huge segments of our personal history if we were to remove grief. This is untenable for anyone who has understood that grief is ultimately an expression of our love for the person who is dead. We grieve because we love. Grief is nothing to be ashamed of. It is not something to get rid of. Rather it is part of what it means to live and to love. Grief is not something we should leave behind. Grief is a precious expression of the love we carry forward forever. We must learn to appreciate grief for what it is and to learn to live with it, by integrating it into our lives.

Grief Is an Expression of Love

It is many years since Ulrike died. The acute pain that flooded my emotions immediately after her death is no longer as sharp and overwhelming as it was. The pain is getting milder, and yet I am constantly reminded of her. There is hardly a day when I don't think of her in one form or another. Often these memories sneak up unexpectedly. I open a book and find a handwritten note from her reminding me how much she loved to read. I hear a song, that she liked very much, and I remember her beautiful alto voice. I look at some family photos where she was still part of us, and I am reminded that she was the very heart and soul of our home. I meet a person who suddenly shares a wonderful or funny story about her, and I remember her pleasant and cheerful laughter. I see a picture by one of her favorite artists, and I remember the lovely artist village of Worpswede in northern Germany, where we spent a few wonderful days during a family vacation. I sing a hymn at church and suddenly I blink back tears because it resonates with my experience with her and with God. I smell a certain perfume and must think of her. I plan my next vacation and remember things she loved

Myths of Closure

to do. I cook a simple meal and admire her far superior cooking skills. I read an inspiring passage in a book and want to share my thoughts with her. I see a beautiful dress and think: that would have been her style, and wonder how she would look in it. When I must make an important decision, I wonder what she would think about this. The list is endless. The incidents that remind me of her are as numerous as the love that created those countless moments that make life beautiful and interesting and challenging.

Should it surprise me that many years later I think of her almost every day? No! Not at all! We were just too close. How could I ever forget her? Some might feel I am stuck in my grief and that I need closure so that I can move on. I don't feel that I am stuck in my grief. I am a happy person. I really live a delightful life. I love my sons and daughter-in-law. I have a fulfilling and satisfying career that challenges me to learn new things and to grow in knowledge and skills. I like the cultural diversity and beauty of people I have met in my travels to more than fifty countries around the world. I enjoy the company of a few very good and close friends. I am content and mostly very happy. Yes, I miss my wife. Why shouldn't I? It makes sense to me. She was my first love. She is the mother of my children. I still love her. Will we ever stop loving silently those we once loved out loud?

Closure is a popular concept in our society. A loved one dies, and we are told we need to find closure. School shootings happen and the community looks for closure. When something tragic happens, we are told we need to get over it and find closure. Although people mean different things when they talk about closure[1] and even though there is no one definition, a common interpretation is: there must be an end to our grief, a finality to the bad thing that happened. Some people have told me that I must get over it, that I must move on, I must find closure. As if grieving is a process that is neatly divided into different stages[2] that you pass through and finally leave behind. Once you have reached that point and live without grief, then everything is well and good.

---

1. Some say it's about forgetting; others use it for peace and forgiveness, and others use closure when talking about revenge and vengeance.

2. In 1969 Elisabeth Kübler-Ross identified five stages in the grieving process (see the commemorative edition of her book, Kübler-Ross and Kessler, *On Grief and Grieving*). This theory of grieving has so successfully found its way into common parlance that many take it as gospel, worrying that something is wrong with them if they don't experience each stage. For many years, I taught these stages to my students when we talked about counseling people who experience bereavement. My own experience has taught me that life is far more complex and recently a number of grief experts have challenged some of the standardized stages.

Love Is!

But this is not how life and grief work. Yes, life goes on. But life is not the same. What we need to understand is the crucial connection between love and grief.

We experience grief only because we have experienced love. We grieve over our loss because we loved that person. We do not grieve for people we do not know personally, or for people we do not love. When tens of thousands of people die in war or some catastrophic event, they are statistics. If one person dies whom we know, it is a tragedy.[3] The stronger our love for this person, the more intense is our grief. Our grief tells us that we dared to love, that we allowed another person to enter the very core of our human being and find a home in our heart. Our grief is proportional to the depth to which someone we love has touched our life. Grieving by its very nature confirms worth. It is only when we understand our grief as an expression of our love that we gain a helpful and healing perspective of how to process it. This is true no matter whether you stay single or remarry. The memory of your love remains. Love is! Love does not want to be left behind! Love does not want to "move on"! Love is there. True love wants to be there—with the other—forever! To expect to leave this behind and forget about it would mean to forget and ignore our love. In a similar manner grief as an expression of our love is simply there. It does not "move on." It is a genuine expression of our love, and it is part of our life. To "move on," to leave grief behind, would be a betrayal of our love. Instead of "moving on" and "forgetting" our grief, or being consumed by it, we need to learn to live with it in healing ways. We can integrate grief into our lives if we learn to see it as part of our love. Grief is love that seeks a place to express our feelings for the person we miss. We will continue to live, and we will continue to grieve, because we continue to love! And genuine love, we are told in Scripture, does not end (1 Cor 13:13). Our grief and the love that fuels it will shift and change and acquire new expressions. It will surface in different ways, but our love and our grief will remain. We don't have to move on from it. We don't have to leave it behind. Love is. This love will be with us as we learn to build the next stages of our life. This love will be with us as we continue to grow and discover the many facets of beauty that still exist. This love will be with us as we discern new ways of living without forgetting. There is therefore no time limit to grief. The good news is: Grief lasts as long as love lasts!

3. Josef Stalin (1879–1953), the general secretary of the Communist Party of the Soviet Union's Central Committee from 1922 until his death in 1953, who ruled the country with dictatorial control, supposedly said: "The death of one man is a tragedy; the death of millions is a statistic." Stalin, "Stalin Quotes."

Chapter 10

Learning Lessons

Accepting Help

IT IS ONE THING to learn to deal with the stressful situations caused by death. Learning to accept help in this process is quite something else. When Ulrike died, I was surprised and touched to experience the wave of help offered by family and friends in the aftermath of her death. We received some help while she was struggling to battle her cancer. Now, I discovered the significant difference between help and *helpful help*. It is relatively easy to offer help. This is quickly done. It requires more thoughtful consideration to provide *helpful help*. Offering help and delivering *helpful help* is not the same thing! *Helpful help* requires active thinking and creativity put into practice with thoughtfulness. *Helpful help* is mindful of the situation and sensitive to the needs of the grieving person. We all need *helpful help* in our lives. What is even more difficult to learn, however, is to accept help when it is offered. This was perhaps one of the most difficult and humbling lessons to learn, at a time when I needed it most.

I learned this lesson in a remarkable way shortly after Ulrike's death. One of the really *helpful helps* came from the wife of a good friend who understood one of my big challenges as I navigated daily life alone. When Ulrike died our youngest son, Daniel, was only eleven years old, Florian was sixteen, and Jonathan was nineteen. Jonathan had just moved to another city to study architecture. Florian and Daniel were still with me. I read

Love Is!

somewhere that one of the most important emotionally stabilizing factors for younger children who have lost a parent is having a continuity of familiar daily routines. In this pattern of familiar routines, the remaining parent becomes the person they become most attached to and relate most closely to. For me, family mealtimes were a key factor in maintaining a familiar daily routine and enabled personal communication. Lunch was the time when we ate and socialized together around our large kitchen table. The school generously offered to let me and my sons eat lunch at the school's cafeteria. While this would save me precious time in preparing meals, it would not give me the privacy and personal quality time with my sons that I would have at home. My difficulty in providing this space of refuge for my children was significantly increased by the fact that I am not a good and experienced cook. I know how to cook spaghetti and I have never burned any water but to prepare a tasty, well balanced, and healthy diet requires an amazing level of organization, skill, and thorough planning. You need to manage the logistics of coordinating what to prepare first and in what sequence in order to have a complete and hot meal ready to eat. When I had to do this by myself, I quickly gained a deeper appreciation of what Ulrike had done so seemingly effortlessly and with great dedication for many years. Looking back, I realize that I should have expressed my sincere appreciation for all her cooking and baking skills more often. But there I was, struggling to provide a warm, healthy meal for us while still teaching full time. On my busiest teaching days, there was a very small window of time to fix lunch after class and before my sons had to attend school again in the afternoon. This was when the wife of my best friend came up with some really *helpful help*. She simply said: "I heard that you have decided to eat at home so that you can have quality time with your sons and can maintain a certain family routine. I really like that idea! I have an idea I'd like to share with you. Tell me, what are your three busiest days of the week and what time do you normally eat together?" I replied: "Monday, Wednesday, and Thursday. We normally eat around 1 PM." "Very well, then," she said, "I will organize with friends and members of our local church, to bring you a full meal, including dessert, every Monday, Wednesday, and Thursday around 1 PM! You don't have to do anything. You don't have to call anybody. I'll organize everything. The food will be delivered to your door. You don't have to open the door. You don't have to talk to anybody who brings the food. You don't have to do anything, except enjoy the meal! Once you have finished eating, just place the empty dishes in front of your door the next day around noon and someone will come by and pick them up. Again, you don't have to talk to anybody. Just leave them there and we will take care of it!" Now, that was really *helpful help* for all of us. I appreciated that I did not have to talk to anybody. Often, I simply was not in the mood to talk. Sometimes I just wanted to be left alone and did not want to see anybody. But to have the food delivered to our home was such a blessing. What was an even greater blessing was that this "heavenly" ministry continued for my three most intense workdays for more than three months! It is said that the first three months are the roughest. During the first months, you struggle the most in establishing some new routine, and often you struggle to simply survive somehow. This help was so thoughtful, and it was really, really helpful. The blessing of this cooking ministry continued in a reduced form during my busiest times at work for over two years! Now, that was dedication! This was *helpful help* for me. Not only was the food a huge blessing, but it also made me realize how deeply other people cared for me and my family.

To receive help means you must be willing to accept help as it is offered. For us, this meant appreciating the generosity and willingness of others to help us and not complaining if some things were not prepared or seasoned in the way we preferred. You must be willing to accept the help that is offered. Otherwise, you cannot enjoy it or will not enjoy it for a long time.

Being willing to accept help also meant making myself a bit more vulnerable than I normally would be with people who did not belong to my immediate family. When another friend offered to pay for a person to come one day a week to clean our apartment, I had to be willing to admit this person into the privacy of my not-so-clean home. I had to be willing to let this person see the messiness of our apartment, which otherwise no one would see. Without that vulnerability, I would not have been able to experience the blessing of this help. Times of crisis and loss allow us to learn to offer *helpful help* to those in need and it also gave me an opportunity to learn to accept help. These experiences taught me the beauty that grows out of caring friendship. It also made me appreciate much more the social and supportive network that I am blessed with through the fellowship of church and family.

Love Is!

Accepting the Reality of Death

Dealing with the reality of death required learning on many fronts. Accepting the reality of Ulrike's death was even more difficult. During the first couple of days and weeks after she had died, her death appeared surreal. On the one hand, my mind knew the truth of her death. I had seen and touched her lifeless, senseless body in the hospital. But the harsh reality of what I had heard and seen only slowly sunk in. During the first couple of days, I noticed that my wishful thinking was not in sync with reality. At times I felt as if she would walk through the door and be with us again. It all seemed like a really bad dream. It was like a horror movie where you long for a happy ending. Of course, there was no happy ending. It could not happen. She was dead. My mind knew what my heart struggled to accept. The longer the reality of her physical absence continued the more real the finality of her death became. Then came the funeral. The act of saying a last "goodbye" at the cemetery, and the moment when her coffin was lowered into the ground, all confirmed the grim reality that my mind knew, but my heart had difficulty accepting. I think it is a blessing that we were not alone during those sad moments. The company of friends, family, and people who knew her and expressed their condolences made the reality of her death even more final. They were also a source of strength. Mourning and grieving her loss together helped me to slowly fathom what had happened. To experience the reality of loss through formal and informal rituals gives structure to the turmoil of our soul and helps carry us through some of our most difficult times. While some funeral rituals are old traditions that have evolved over time, I experienced them in new ways when Ulrike was buried. I think it is meaningful to have good rituals and customs to guide us in those raw moments of saying goodbye. They signify what happened and provide some context of faith in which to put our loss. Sometimes the simplest moments hold the most profound truth.[1]

Shortly after her funeral the school where Ulrike and I had worked and the church to which we belonged organized a special memorial service. People expressed their appreciation for Ulrike, and we provided an opportunity for the larger community to also express their gratitude and grief. Hearing specific incidences that people fondly remembered, things for which they were grateful, moments they felt blessed by her presence,

---

1. Hickman, *Healing after Loss*, June 30.

her words, and acts of kindness were healing balm for my wounded heart. It showed me that she was not forgotten and was appreciated by many.

The real struggle and difficulty in dealing with her death only emerged in the following weeks and months! It is one thing to mentally acknowledge the reality of her death—it is an altogether different ballgame to accept this harsh reality as part of *my* life.

I still distinctly remember the moment when I realized what that meant for me. Was I willing to accept the loss of my wife as part of my life?! This was not something I had wished for. This was not how I had envisioned the second part of my life. This was not planned. This was not my fault. Yet, it had become part of *my* life. To accept that my life now was a life without Ulrike, to accept that her death had become part of my story, was not easy.

It was tempting to remain in an illusory state of mind, a make-believe world, in which I did not allow the reality of her loss to really be part of my life. It seemed far easier to repress that painful reality and feeling. Only when I had the courage to face my denial and honestly faced the painful reality of her absence in my life, with what it implied, was I able to cautiously order my everyday life anew without her. When I abandoned my inner resistance and accepted the new reality of being without my spouse, I cried. At the same time, a heavy load was lifted off my shoulders. It was as if God lifted me up and gave me wings that helped me soar like the eagles. My decision to accept the reality of her death as part of my biography did not answer all my questions. But it helped me to see that this has made my life unique and distinguishes me from everyone else. This is not a once and for all decision. It is rather something that I must acquire anew in ever changing circumstances and temptations. It is a learning process that, I guess, will last for the rest of my life.

Living by Faith and God's Grace

Of course, as a single parent and man I have personal needs and longings that cannot easily be stilled. There is a great temptation to pursue a path that might bring quick pleasure but no lasting satisfaction and happiness. This is not blessed by God. Here I learned—and I am still learning—what it means to trust God, day by day, and to live by faith. To live your life by faith in God alone is easy to say but difficult to do. It is something that requires attention and constant, deliberate decisions to deal with the myriads of temptations that try to lure me away from trusting God's goodness and care. I will not succeed in modeling my life by faith in God if I try to fabricate the solution to my problems on my own terms. I need to learn to trust God and his truly amazing grace more fully in every area of my life, even if I don't see how, humanly speaking, he will ever be able to meet all my needs. I have to remind myself that God has a thousand ways to help of which I know nothing (Jer 33:3). This is something that I cannot adequately explain in words, but I can testify that I have repeatedly experienced it in my own life. Trusting God and his grace and goodness, and to be connected with him, is what really counts in our process of waiting and grieving. What resonates with this experience is an inner longing of the soul. Longing is a delightful word. Human beings are never more human than when we see them longing for someone or something. There is a certain sparkle and fire in their eyes. Full of expectation. Longing is a word that leads us out of a narrow mindset and a dry spirit of ritual performance. Things that happen out of a deep longing are happening with the authority of the heart. In our longing, the whole human being is involved. Longing is something you cannot command to happen. Rather it grows and blossoms in the soil of love: it is free and never forced. The person who longs is not satisfied with things as they are but tries to change things to the better, while in the meantime living a joyful and faithful life by God's grace alone, amidst all pain and suffering. As such I long to see the day when Jesus comes again, when God's great love will ultimately prove stronger even than death, and when he will resurrect those who have trusted him fully! Then God will wipe away every tear from our eyes and "there will be no more death, nor sorrow, nor crying. There will be no more pain" (Rev 21:4 NKJV). And yet, this future reality is not what I experience in the here and now. Today, there are times where the physical absence of Ulrike makes me cry and painfully reminds me that we are not in heaven yet.

The Sadness of the Resurrection

Some people, especially those who believe in God, would tell me that I didn't need to be sad and depressed because we have the hope of the resurrection. We have the promise that we will see each other again, hopefully soon. I guess many uttered these words with the best intentions. I firmly believe that I will see Ulrike again on the resurrection morning when Jesus Christ will come again, and the words of the apostle Paul become a jubilant and joyful reality: "For the Lord himself will come down from heaven, with a loud command, with the voice of the archangel and with the trumpet call of God, and the dead in Christ will rise first. After that, we who are still alive and are left will be caught up together with them in the clouds to meet the Lord in the air. And so we will be with the Lord forever. Therefore encourage each other with these words" (1 Thess 4:16–18 NIV). I believe there will be a resurrection of the dead. I know that Ulrike put her trust in Jesus Christ, and we will see each other again. Yet, these words sometimes made me angry and sad, when I heard them, especially when people uttered them rather thoughtlessly. Why? Because in the moment of great loss the thought of seeing Ulrike sometime in the future was not a comfort. I dearly missed her now! I missed her support now. I missed her counsel now. I missed her gentle touch now. I missed her inspiring presence now. I did not want the prospect of some future bliss—I wanted her here and now! When we are affected by pain and grief, we quickly realize that the promise of a future resurrection and reunion does not eliminate the pain of her absence now. This is not how life functions. Believers go through the same emotions of grief as nonbelievers. Grief is a reality that is part of our human existence. It is part of our human nature. Those who say that we should not grieve the loss of a loved person have never understood the nature of love and the enormous hole that is left in our hearts and minds when a loved one dies. The deeper the love, the stronger the grief. Just as it takes time to heal from major surgery, it takes time to heal from the loss of a loved one. There will always be a certain void in our lives, and the pain that accompanies it, just as we will always have a scar that reminds us of a major surgery. This grieving process is something that you cannot speed up. It requires time. A person who has learned to live with grief in her own life once told me that processing the loss of a person is like going through a house with many windows. Every window represents a memorable experience with the person we love, a special place both liked, something they shared or enjoyed. Every view through such a window of memory needs to be processed now alone before I can close it and open a new window while venturing into something new in my life without my partner. This process takes time and cannot be fast-forwarded. The many different facets of life, with their rich variety, take time to process, and cannot be mastered quickly. I initially hesitated to approach some of our favorite places alone. It took time before I was able to handle these "confrontations." It was painful to think of experiencing the beauty of those places alone and not to be able to share my feelings and thoughts with her. Even when I finally dared to visit those places alone it was not the same and it required time to adjust to my new reality. It took determination to find new ways of dealing with it. Healing takes place when I begin to integrate the multifaceted aspects of grief and beauty into my new life without the physical presence of the person I loved. That is why some people say that you need to spend at least one year, i.e., all four seasons, alone to experience the reality of the annual flow of time from a new perspective. Learning not to ignore my grief, but to acknowledge it and grieve well with it, made me realize that this is one of the best ways of honoring my deceased loved one. But grieving is not just an experience that affects my passage through time. It also affects my identity. It affects who I am.

Who Am I? Searching for Identity

Losing my spouse forced me to experience many things that were new to me. One question that affected me more drastically had to do with my new identity as a widower. To be quite honest I still don't like the word and what it does to me. It certainly left me wondering who I was, partly perhaps because I was confronted with a new social standing in society. Who am I now—without her? Where is my place? What is my role? Who are my peers now? Who is the social group that I belong to? *Who am I now?*

The importance of this question becomes visible in seemingly little details that almost appear insignificant to a person not affected by loss through death. I was confronted with this question when I had to fill in new application forms for my bank accounts (we had enjoyed shared bank accounts), when I had to apply for new legal documents, or even when I requested some international travel information. I had to check whether I was married or single or widowed. Perhaps you wonder why this even matters: "married or single?" Many documents do not even have the third category, widowed. Married or single are the only two options and they leave me somewhat confused and disoriented. I wonder: am I married? Am I *still* married? Or am I single now? Ulrike is dead, so I guess that means that I am not married anymore. But I still *feel* married and connected to her. In my thoughts and my feelings, she is still my wife. So, I can't bring myself to check the category "single." It feels like a lie to me or like a betrayal. But it is even more complicated than that.

Learning Lessons

Yes, I am single. I am a single parent now. But am I not a single parent who is single because I got divorced or I never married in the first place. I encountered this dilemma several times, especially when people inquired whether I am married. When they found out that I had children but was single, they almost always thought that I was divorced. Yes, I am a single parent now, but I am not divorced. So, who am I? I was committed to Ulrike for my entire life. I shared my most private thoughts and intimate feelings with her. With her I learned so many new things that helped me become a better person. With her my life was complete. Without Ulrike—I was wondering, who am I now?

I am a widower. But being a widower is not something to brag about. *Widower* is not an attractive word! It certainly is not a compliment. At least not for me. I still don't like the sound of it. Could it be that we have forgotten to speak about being a widower or being single as something that can be successfully mastered and even enjoyed by God's power and grace? Married people need certain interpersonal skills and God's forgiveness, grace, and help to bond and grow in their marriage relationship. And we need the same when we are single, divorced, or experience bereavement. To be married to the right partner—and being the right partner for your spouse—is a wonderful thing and can be a little like heaven on earth. But I also know, it is no sin to stay single! Jesus, our great example, never married. Paul, the greatest missionary of the early church and a powerful apostle, lived single and either never married or was a widower who remained single after his wife died. Perhaps we have to learn to rediscover that God's grace is fully sufficient for any marriage as well as for anyone who stays single for whatever reason.

When I pondered the question "Who am I without a spouse?" I was reminded of an answer that Dietrich Bonhoeffer gave in a poem he wrote in his prison cell when he was confronted with this important question for himself after he was confined and sentenced to death for his involvement in attempting to assassinate Hitler.[2] Contemplating all the uncertainty and pressure around him, and being fully cognizant of the competing temptations, challenges, and dire prospects that confronted him, the imprisoned Bonhoeffer asked the question: "Who am I?" Bonhoeffer's answer is as

---

2. For an insightful and well written account of Bonhoeffer's remarkable life and the unpredictable and little-known circumstances of his last days, that almost let him escape his imprisonment, see Metaxas, *Bonhoeffer*.

profound as it is simple. He writes: "Who am I? They mock me, these lonely questions of mine. Whoever I am, thou knowest me; O God, I am thine!"[3]

While many factors influence and shape my identity and compete for my attention, I am once again reminded that my identity is not determined by the circumstances that surround me or the things that affect me. My ultimate identity is grounded in my relationship with God. I belong to God. He knows me and he is my salvation. God is the foundation of my hope. He is the faithful guide who will not leave me nor forsake me. And while I am alone now, without my wife, I am not lonely with him at my side. He is the source of my strength that keeps me going. He is the one who refreshes my soul in ways that I cannot even adequately describe with words. But I can only testify that it is very real.

But what do you do when the pain of loss is sheer unbearable?

Numbing the Pain

Have you ever wondered why many people start addictive habits after they experience great pain? Why do people look for distractions in any shape and form when they go through periods of intense suffering? Why does the death of a person we love with all our heart so easily trigger destructive patterns that are toxic to a healthy life?

The pain in losing a person you love is horrific. In many ways the pain of such loss is sheer unbearable. It is not easy to live with an emotional void in your heart. There is an emptiness that affects every level of your existence. To suffer the physical absence of the person you love is incredibly difficult to endure. Life appears so meaningless, pointless, purposeless without the person you love. The daily routine of self-care that once occupied much of your attention now appeared so unimportant, even futile. The will to live vanishes. The purpose to live fades way. The pain is massive. The wound cuts so deep. You literally feel the soreness from the loss all over your body. The physiological and health reactions of your body can have severe physical reactions. The hurt of the heart is physically and emotionally draining and sucks every energy out of your body. It completely depletes you. It makes you numb, and often leaves you depressed. It is a psychological injury of gigantic proportions. You feel devastated as if a hurricane has mercilessly plowed through your protected life, leaving a track of devastation behind. Or compare it to a tsunami that has flooded your life

---

3. Bonhoeffer, *Letters*, 460.

and left everything crushed and in rubble. It is like a blazing fire that leaves your heart and soul in ashes. It is like an earthquake that has shaken your very foundation and sense of security. And sometimes it feels as if all of the above has happened at the same time.

Many cannot bear the pain of emptiness and try to drown the feelings of loneliness. They turn to addictive activities to numb the pain to make life more bearable. People try to anaesthetize themselves through alcohol or drugs, overeating, hoarding, cleaning, spending money, gambling, or whatever it is, that prevents the unbearable reality of emptiness from intruding on your life. We all have our favorite ways of protecting ourselves and have become skilled at hiding the emotional hurt we experience. However, just because my form of denial is more productive or more socially acceptable does not fundamentally make it any healthier on an emotional level, or more honest about what I am really feeling under the outside cover that others see. Some men secretly become slaves of pornography in the feeble and futile attempt to find something they no longer can enjoy and experience with their marriage partner. Others suppress the pain and try to block it out by getting distracted with their work. They easily escape the harsh reality of being alone by becoming workaholics, another addictive and destructive behavior. Others plunge rather quickly into new relationships without having given themselves the much-needed time to grieve, grow, and heal. They appear haunted and strangely driven to hastily pursue a new relationship, because they simply cannot bear the pain of living alone. Not a few have regretted to have rushed into a new liaison with another person for which they really were not ready yet. Let's face it: a wrong relationship will make you feel even more alone than when you were single.

All these self-made substitutes do not truly satisfy. They cannot fill the emptiness that is left by the death of a loved one. Substitutes do not lead to a fulfilled life. These feelings of loss, emptiness, and grief do not disappear. They seem to be permanent. Rather than numbing the pain or denying the reality of loss the challenge is to learn to live with it and through it.

I do not claim to have mastered it all. Nor do I have an easy solution for all the struggles we face when we are confronted with death. But let me say this: Be gentle with yourself! Let's not be judgmental when someone else is going through a crisis. The thought of living all those years ahead of me without Ulrike was tough and utterly unbearable. It triggered feelings of panic and intense stress. When I attempted to think too far into my future without her, I quickly got nervous, and feelings of panic threatened to overwhelm me. I did not have the strength to even think about it.

Remember, we live our lives in moments, not years. The future might look scary and stretches out endlessly in front of you. The future will have aspects of emptiness, but if *this* moment is wonderful, *this* delightful moment with good friends, *this* unexpected smile that greets you, *this* walk in the woods, *this* gorgeous sunset that colors the evening sky, *this* lovely exchange with a child, *this* cup of tea (or hot chocolate or whatever it is that you enjoy drinking), *this* exquisite taste of delicious fruit or dessert, if *this* moment is wonderful and beautiful, then savor it. In moments of grief, the long view can be overwhelming. What we need to learn is to cherish and experience *this* moment for itself, without being bound hostage to the past or scared of an uncertain future.

A thought that helped me regain this hopeful perspective and has enabled me to trust and treasure life for its simple beauties is Jesus' teaching when he said: "Don't worry about tomorrow, for tomorrow will bring its own worries. Today's trouble is enough for today" (Matt 6:34 NLT). Or as Eugene Peterson puts it in *The Message*: "Don't get worked up about what may or may not happen tomorrow. God will help you deal with whatever hard things come up when the time comes" (Matt 6:34 The Message). Immediately prior to these words Jesus gently reminds us that all our worrying will not add one single day to the span of our lives. Worry and fear do not need to dominate our thinking. Our heavenly father knows everything we need (Matt 6:32–33). He promised to provide if we trust him! This has been my experience. Humanly speaking I cannot explain it, but I can testify that the words of Lam 3:22–23 are true: "God's steadfast love never ceases, and his compassions never fail. They are new every morning" (ESV). Perhaps even greater than the pain of loss that I experienced is God's amazing grace and steadfast love that have given me the strength to carry on, one step at a time. Often, I literally could not bear to think more than a week or a month ahead without getting anxious and quite nervous. I could not envision how life would be a year from now. God always gave me enough strength for the next step, for the next day, and sometimes the next hour was all I could handle. But then this is all I needed. And it is all that he provided. Sometimes we want God to light up our path all the way from the beginning to our final destination like a strong laser-like flashlight lights up our path. That is not how it works. I often do not see the end from the beginning. God does. He knows. God has given me enough light and

Learning Lessons

strength to take the next necessary step to move forward. If I was willing to walk it in faith, trusting his goodness, being steeped in his provisions, and not worrying about missing out, I found that my everyday human concerns were graciously and amazingly met, one step at a time.

Chapter 11

Lovingly Moving Forward

Love Creates a Memory No One Can Steal

SHORTLY AFTER ULRIKE'S FUNERAL, I received a letter from a student who had lost her father early in her life. Knowing the experience of loss and pain firsthand, she wrote words that went beyond the typical words of condolence I received from many others. In her personal letter she quoted an Irish proverb that had become significant to her and since has become very meaningful to me. The proverb goes something like this:

> Death leaves a heartache no one can heal.
> Love leaves a memory no one can steal![1]

How true these words are! Indeed, death leaves a sorrow no one can heal. But let us not forget that love creates a memory no one can steal! Yes, love created countless memories in my life. Our love for each other created many memories that no one can take from me. Memories that enrich my life. Memories for which I will always be grateful. Memories that I will never forget. It is good to remember those moments when love created something that lingers on, that stays alive, that connects me with the person I love. Besides the many memories that love has created in my life and that has given my life a quality that nothing else could have given it, our three sons, Jonathan, Florian, and Daniel, are a living reminder of our love

1. Good News Network, "Quote of the Day."

for each other. Because they are literally the product of our love, it gave me a strong impulse to carry on and show them my enduring love for them. They would not exist, were it not for our love. While I cannot replace the love of my wife for them and they acutely miss their mother, they know that I deeply love them, all of them, and will always love them. Love binds us together. Love creates a bond that is stronger even than death. This leads me to my next point. Love has a little sister: her name is hope.

Love Has a Little Sister: Her Name Is Hope

Bible-believing Christians have the hope that one day soon, when Jesus comes again in glory, he will bring with him the reward he has promised to those who put their trust in him. From heaven he will come to judge the living and the dead, the Apostles' Creed states. This is the moment when the graves will burst open and the dead in Christ will be resurrected to new and eternal life. This is the moment when God's love will prove stronger even than death. This is the moment when death—the last enemy (1 Cor 15:26)—will be conquered. This is the moment when there will be a jubilant reunion with those who were separated by death. This hope is born in faith. Hope is the little sister of love. Love creates this hope. Love, the Bible tells us, ultimately wins. Jesus is victor! His *death* on the cross has opened the door to our resurrection. And his resurrection sealed the certainty of our resurrection. For if there is no resurrection of the dead, then our faith is in vain (1 Cor 15:13–14). But through Jesus' death and resurrection death is swallowed up in victory (1 Cor 15:54). This hope is vibrant. This hope we have when Jesus Christ is the Lord of our life. This hope will never disappoint. It is a sure foundation.

The Beauty of Tears

Feelings of great joy and especially intense feelings of abysmal grief and pain bring forth tears. Remembering precious moments and shared experiences can water your eyes and make you cry. It is not wrong to cry! Tears are perfectly all right. Jesus cried when his good friend Lazarus died (John 11:35). When David's son Absalom died, David cried (2 Sam 19:4). Tears are mini messengers. Tears are those little drops of humanity that often tell with the greatest possible tenderness what words cannot adequately express. They stand ready twenty-four hours a day. Often tears are an alternative or substitute for words that are stuck in our throats. They drip and drop from the bottom of our hearts, and powerfully communicate the deepest emotions that we as human beings are capable to express. When words are helpless and sound shallow and superficial, tears are there to express our deepest sympathy, grief, sorrow, and also our joy! God has created us with the ability to weep. And God is touched by our tears. God is not indifferent to my sorrow and my joy. God knows every single tear I have shed. And *he* knows the reason for it. In Ps 56:8 it says:

> You keep track of all my sorrows.
> You have collected all my tears in your bottle.
> You have recorded each one in your book. (NLT)

God knows our tears and he understands. Someone once told me: "not he is the closest friend to you, who laughs with you and enjoys a good time. The closest friend you will find is he, who weeps with you!" Sharing the grief with your tears brings a healing touch and it bonds you with the person with whom you weep. It reminds me of the words of the apostle Paul, who wrote: "Rejoice with those who rejoice, weep with those who weep" (Rom 12:15 NASB).

Chapter 12

Don't Say It!

WHILE IT IS GOOD and a blessing to express our thoughts and feelings in words of love and appreciation and while it is good to share the grief of others in our tears, we live in a world that tries hard to ignore the pain and reality of death until it is on your doorstep. We frequently don't know what to say when confronted with death's harsh reality. It often leaves us speechless, and when we say something, it often does not seem to be the right thing. To speak the right words at the right time is precious. "An idea well expressed is like a design of gold, set in silver" (Prov 24:11 GNT). Words can comfort and heal. They can become precious treasures. But words carelessly uttered and thoughtlessly spoken can easily have the opposite effect.

There are some words that grieving people do not need to hear. Before I address some of those undesirable verbal expressions let's remember that what people need most are not our words of wisdom. They need our practical help and calm presence. Just being there *with them*, silently sharing the pain of their loss, attentively listening to the unexplainable and deeply perplexing things of life, without trying to give a reason for this tragedy or an explanation for everything that happened, is the best we can offer. It is not easy to do just that, in moments like these. Instead, we are tempted to quickly explain things that do not make much sense to us. So, remember, talking is always completely optional, especially when we are tempted to quickly give some good advice. What Job's friends did first is perhaps the greatest comfort and gift they could give him as he experienced the tragic loss of his wealth, health, and the loss of the life of his children: they sat *with him in silence* (see Job 2:13).

Being silent does not mean doing nothing. Job's friends were silent, but they did something very important! They offered their silent presence, their company. They offered themselves. They listened. To put it in simple terms: they were there. This often is the very thing people need most when they mourn. They need our supportive presence. This is what I needed. I needed people who did not ignore me in my grief, but who were simply there. People who gave me a call, who gave me a hug or an encouraging tap on my shoulder. These people, I call them friends, who endured my painful awkwardness and shared the grief I felt. A shared grief is half the burden. A shared burden has a magnetic power to draw us together. Why? Because in crisis situations life's pain is endured better in the fellowship and comfort of friends. It creates community. Be a person who attentively and patiently listens. Be a person who hears the indescribable pain and who endures the myriads of unanswered questions. Don't be afraid to shed a tear with the person who mourns.

Be also a person who is open to listen to God. I believe he can guide you in what to say and, more than that, he can give you the patience and humility to know when it is better to be quiet. Frequently what comforts people more than any answers to unanswerable questions is the experience of our empathy. Empathy begins with an act of imagination. To meet someone who allows the death of the other person to affect them is a healing balm to the wounded soul. To know a person who is touched by what has happened to those who mourn and who makes himself vulnerable by weeping with those who shed tears can be a great comfort and blessing.

But then the moment comes when we will talk. There are a few things I think we better not say to a person who is grieving.[1] There are grief statements that do not land well, at least they didn't for me. But do not be too hard on yourself if you have said any of the following statements. I have fallen in the same trap myself. Grieving loss is one of the hardest things to experience and it is equally challenging to support someone in it and even harder to find the right words. Here are a few things that were thrown at me after I lost my wife that I felt were not very helpful.

---

1. Some of the following thoughts are taken from McInerny, *Young Widows Club*, 52–53.

Don't Say It!

"It could be worse"

Please don't say that! Who are you comparing my loss to? This is as if my loss is not recognized for what it really is to me. For me, this was one of the worst responses I have received. When you talk to a grieving person don't compare his or her grief with that of another human being. Every loss of life and every grieving is unique and should be acknowledged as such.

"This is what you need to do"

Unsolicited advice about how one should be grieving is another no go. If you start with: "You should be" please STOP. Grieving is personal and everyone is dealing with their loss in their own way. Everyone can master a grief it seems, as long as it is not his or her own! Grief does not have a strict timeline. Every grief has its own timetable which only the griever knows. It is foolish to think or to expect to get over a serious grief quickly. When I think I know better than the grieving person when to grieve, how to grieve, and when to move on, it puts me in the position where I give unsolicited advice, which can be quite painful and cause a lot of stress. Before jumping in to "help" first ASK if they are interested in some information. When Ulrike was ill, we had people sending us links to YouTube videos and offering recommendations for treatments that they believed were helpful without even fully knowing the kind of cancer Ulrike had. After her death some offered similar advice why this might have happened to her and to me, and what I needed to do to deal with it. I felt this was not very sensitive and it irritated and confused me even more.

"Everything happens for a reason"

Be careful with this one! There are some things that happen in this sinful and imperfect world without any perceivable or good reason. I firmly believe that God knows everything and knows so much more than we created beings will ever know and understand. But precisely because we are not God and because we created human beings lack his omniscience, I also believe that we don't know the reason for everything that happens. This fact should make us humble and cautious not to come up with self-fabricated reasons why some things happen to us. After all, how can we pretend to be omniscient—only God is. It seems that human beings often come up with reasons so that we can deal more easily with something that otherwise would be very difficult for us to bear and to endure—unanswered questions. Some of the toughest situations I faced came from pious people who attempted to answer why Ulrike got cancer and died: "she must have had unresolved conflicts that were the cause of her cancer"; or "you did not have enough faith in God when you prayed, otherwise she would have been healed!"; or "now you can be so much more empathetic with other people who also suffer loss"; and the list goes on. These "answers" only intensified my problem. Now I was not only confronted with my grief and how to deal with it but I was also told that I had not had enough faith in God. How insensitive, I thought! I was told that her death was necessary for God to teach me more compassion as if God would not have other means to teach me that!

I firmly believe that we must learn to live with some open questions. As committed Christians, I also think we have to learn not to waver, but to trust God's goodness and grace, despite our open questions. More important than knowing all the answers is knowing and trusting the One who knows, even though I don't have all the answers. It certainly takes faith to believe in miracles, but it requires no less faith to continue to trust God when no miracle occurs.

"At least you have"

Don't start any phrase of "comfort" with the words "at least." No matter how good their life was, no matter how long they have been married, and no matter how old their child was when they lost her, it still hurts that they are gone. I suppose, when people said sentences that started with: "At least you have," they wanted to make me feel better, to comfort me, and take away my pain. It is hard to see another person suffering and in pain. But those people often did not understand that in trying to talk my pain away, they are actually dismissing and minimizing the extent of my feelings. People are quick to make such statements about other people's losses, but I don't think that anybody would welcome and accept them if they were the recipients.

After my wife died, several people said to me: "at least you still have your children!" Yes, I still had my children, and I am grateful for each of them. People said: "At least you are still alive"; "at least Ulrike does not suffer anymore"; "at least you had her for as long as you did." Yes, but that did not make her loss easier for me. If anything, it intensified the pain of her absence. These words of comfort feel especially terrible because there is an implicit second part of that same sentence. People who are grieving can easily fill in that second, silent, part. You could call it a "ghost sentence."[2] The second, silent part of that same sentence often is: "so you don't have to feel the way you feel!"; "stop feeling so sad!"; "stop being so destroyed by this!" Even though people never said it that explicitly, the implied message is still there, and it matters.

It seems that people often used these words in a futile attempt to ease the harshness of my loss. They wanted to console me when I was in pain. I did not find such sentences comforting or helpful. You don't make it easier for the grieving person when you say, "At least you have." As awkward as it might be for you to sense my grief, endure your awkwardness and stay with me anyway. Hang out with me and with my pain. I need your presence, your companionship, not your good advice. "Grief is not a problem to be solved, it is an experience to be carried"[3] and it is carried more easily in the company of good friends and people who understand.

There is another silent message that often goes along with the words: "at least you have." The unspoken message often transmitted is: you *needed* this somehow.[4] "At least this will make you a better person in the end"; "at least you can understand grieving people better now," etc. I cannot deny that I have gained insights into grieving and suffering that I did not have before. What makes me uncomfortable, however, is the unspoken, indirect message that I was not a good person in the first place, and somehow, I needed this tragedy. I needed this painful experience in order to grow and develop. As if loss and hardship are the only way to grow as a human being. As though pain and hardship are the only door to a better, deeper spiritual life, the only way to be truly compassionate and kind. No question, there is always room for improvement in our lives. No one is perfect. We all need to grow. However, even in my grief and pain, this improvement is due to my choices and how I align myself with who I want to be, rather than to what is happening to me.

Sometimes a similar line of reasoning is found among some Christian people who seem to think that God decided that it was time for Ulrike to die and therefore God made it happen. I find this pious sentiment at odds with the Christian gospel and the biblical picture of God. Death is not the

---

2. Devine has pointed that out in her book *It's OK*, 20.
3. Devine, *It's OK*, 24.
4. Devine makes this important observation in her book *It's OK*, 22.

normal instrument of God's dealings with us. Instead, the Bible tells us that death is the last enemy that needs to be abolished (1 Cor 15:26). God will overcome the power of death as our last great enemy. God does not delight in our death. Death causes God to suffer and he shares our suffering. My pain over Ulrike's death is shared by the pain God suffers over *her* death. God desires to make our lives flourish and he wants to give us abundant life (John 10:10), even eternal life. The Bible tells us this is true. Therefore, there must be "at least" something more than death, there must be hope. This "at least" is fully legitimate.

"But"

People said to me: "What you are going through is terrible, *but* this experience will help you to understand other grieving people better." Or: "Now Ulrike is dead, *but* at least you are not all alone, you still have your children." I don't deny that there is some truth to the superficial acknowledgment that what I was going through was terrible. There is an element of truth in that I do understand grieving people better now that I have experienced significant loss in my own life. Yes, my children are still alive. So, technically I was not all alone, although I now was a single parent, which did not make things easier for me. However, such statements were not particularly helpful to me. I don't think that Ulrike had to die for me to develop greater empathy for other people. I did not want to hear how my grief was going to help others when I was still so deeply entrenched in my own. So, if you are tempted to say "I know, *but*" think again if what you want to say is helpful or hold your breath.

"I can't imagine what you are going through"

Sometimes people said to me: "I can't imagine what you are going through!" I have often wondered if they really meant what they said. The truth is our brains automatically begin to imagine when we are confronted with the pain and suffering of another human being.[5] Neurobiologically we are connected to each other and being close to the pain of another human being makes us feel pain. It starts a reaction in us. It might be true that the person who makes such a statement cannot *fully* understand what I am

---

5. Devine, *It's OK*, 41.

going through, yet to hear such a sentence was not particularly helpful for me. Rather than connecting me with the speaker, such a statement created distance between us. I want the people that really love and care for me to imagine what I am going through so that I can feel safe sharing how hard things are for me right now. When someone says: "I can't imagine" it seems as if the person is not even seriously trying to put himself into my shoes. It misses the determination to better understand how I am doing and what I must be feeling. It takes the focus away from the griever who needs support and instead puts the focus on the other person. I think people who say this often just want to help but do not really know what to say. For me, replacing "I can't imagine" with "I don't know what you are going through right now means for you, would you like to talk about it?" feels much more supportive and opens a door for a conversation and dialogue that can be healing.

"I know (exactly) how you feel"

While this phrase is often said in an attempt to connect and empathize, I often wondered if someone could really understand how I felt. After all, their lives and experiences were not identical to mine. What I experienced was singular and unique. If they said: "I have not experienced what you have experienced, and I can only dimly imagine what this must mean for you" I would have believed them more. Sometimes I felt that some people took it too far when they said this and then started reminiscing about their own loss and grief without my asking them to do so. This gave me the impression that it was more about them than about me. Although they let me know that they had "been there," their focus was not really on me, but rather on them and their experience. I didn't find this helpful. There might be an appropriate time to share your own story—later. For now, just show up and be there for me.

"I am here for you. Give me a call if you need anything!"

This sounds so caring, nice, and helpful. But chances are high that a grieving person is not going to reach out to you. It might even be that the grieving person does not really know what he needs. Often, I was not in the mood to talk to anybody. If I would have had the courage to call a person, I did not know if the person was really available at that moment. Usually, I had not the energy to explain myself or even dared to ask. It's not my nature to quickly ask people for help. This did not change in my grief. What I found more helpful was when people creatively thought about what I might enjoy or what might be good for me and then offered specific, tangible support. Of course, this meant that they would actually have to think about what I really needed and then offer it without expecting anything in return.

What I really need is someone who accepts me in all my messiness and unpredictability. At times I seem fine and smiling. This does not mean that this happy moment of being okay can't switch at any point! I might suddenly be reminded of something that makes me sad or leaves me unexplainably grumpy. Don't hold these sudden and spontaneous mood swings against me. Allow for this unpredictability. It is a grieving person's prerogative to change his mood. Don't expect me to know anything about the future. The future terrifies me. The past and the future are too painful for me to reside in for too long. Plans feel meaningless. Memories are painful. Don't be offended if what you offer does not work out perfectly on your first attempt. Don't take it personally. Keep trying. Keep praying for me and pray for a better understanding of what you could do that would be good and *helpful help*. If all this sounds hard—it is because it really is. Dealing with a bereaved person is perhaps the hardest job in the world. Please don't give up!

"I'd better not say anything"

Having read the above reservations some may think that the best option is to say nothing at all. We often do not know what to say or do. Because we are so unsure of what to say, we are easily tempted to think: "I don't want to say the wrong thing!" "I do not want to aggravate the pain." "Therefore, I'd better say nothing." That is why many people stay silent. Please don't let discomfort prevent you from reaching out. It is awkward for the grieving person too. Saying nothing is a terrible thing to do to a grieving person. To hear nothing easily feels like abandonment. It feels as if the dead person is ignored or forgotten. To hear nothing at all makes grieving people feel as if they have not only lost their most loved person, but they have also lost their people too. Which makes them feel even more alone. Now, more than ever, the person who grieves needs your support. Remember, you don't need to have an answer to all their questions, or any of their questions, and you don't need to give any advice. I did not expect another person to make things better, but I needed their support. So don't think you have to be my savior. Speaking and providing comfort in grief can be done with actions in addition to or in place of words. To give a hug. To sit with me in attentive silence. To mow the lawn. To fix the car. To drop off some food without asking. To show up—even when you shut up. To brighten my day with some flowers. These are all things that work very well. There is no limit to thoughtful creativity.

If you want to say something, but don't know what to say, just be honest and say: "I actually don't know what to say in this situation. I don't know exactly what you are going through at the moment, but I just want you to know that you're loved and that I am here for you and that I care for you. I will gladly help you in any way, whatever it is that you need."

Chapter 13

Helpful Help!

Grief Is Not Contagious

SOMETIMES PEOPLE ACT AS if grief is a contagious disease. Even though grief can rub off on you, you can't catch someone's grief like a virus. It might make you uncomfortable and sad. Even if you experience some uncomfortable emotions, showing up for a friend or person you care about means that you love them enough to be with them through their hardest moments. Showing up in whatever capacity you can sends an important signal. If you don't know what to say, show your support in other ways: cook a meal, send a thoughtful care package that can brighten the day, check in to simply say: "I am thinking of you!" Send a handwritten postcard or short letter. Leave a little message of encouragement. In the next section there are a few more practical ideas of what you can ask or do.

Meaningful Time

Here are a few ideas of meaningful ways to spend time with a grieving friend.[1]

---

[1]. But remember, whatever you offer or want to do with them, make it easy for them to refuse if they aren't up to it. Keep it manageable and untaxing. The following list has grown out of my own experience of going through grief and loss and has been inspired by a number of helpful insights from Bates, *Languages of Loss,* 117–23; and Nicola and

- Ask if they would like to go for a walk. Offer to stop by to pick them up. Going on a favorite or new trail, doing a brisk walk while filling your lungs with fresh air, or any exercise in nature can make a positive difference.
- Ask if you could visit the grave or memorial place with them.
- Ask if you could help start a garden, or plant a new flower bed or bulbs, rake leaves, plant a memorial tree or rose bush, or do some work in the yard together.
- Make yourself available to drive the grieving person to church and go to church together. Accompany them in the building and sit with them!
- Ask if you could go to a concert or watch a nice movie together.
- Ask if you can pick them up to go to a nice café or restaurant for breakfast, brunch, dinner, or lunch.
- Make some food—any food (if you can find out what their favorite food is, even better!)—and take it around or have it delivered to them. Don't impose on them while bringing the food. They may not be hungry or may not feel like seeing anyone. Respect that.
- Do the washing up, iron the laundry, walk the dog, feed the cat, entertain the kids . . . use your eyes and see what needs to be done.
- Ask whether you could do the grocery shopping together or browse the sporting goods store for some new activity.
- Invite them to your house for a meal, invite them to a small study group, or include them in a family activity. Don't ask them to join a large social event where they will have to talk or explain themself or attempt to be witty with many other people.
- Bring them a magazine or playlist of some favorite music or a delightful book—something to distract them that is not too taxing.
- Give the grieving person a hug where it is appropriate.
- Write a handwritten note with some encouraging and inspiring words. I still think that handwritten cards and letters are far superior to electronic messages. Something that comes through the letter box makes a massive difference. It gives the grieving person something to

---

Nicola, "Comfort for the Day."

physically open and hold in his hands and keep. If you don't know the postal address, find someone who does. But even an electronic message is better than no message at all. In your note write down some of your memories of the dead person and express why they were important to you. Tell them how you knew the person and how you fit into their life. Positive stories of the deceased are great to hear for grieving people. They long to hear for any stories of their loved one, however minor or out of date! Let them know that you too are impacted by the loss of this important person. Make clear that you do not expect a response. They have enough to deal with.

- Bring some flowers to brighten their day and that will bring some color and beauty to the home, and maybe take a vase. The quantity of flowers during the early stages of loss often exceeds the number of vases found in a normal household.
- Send a little surprise package with some goodies and little things that show your love and let the other person see that you think of her.
- If you have a holiday home somewhere invite them to stay whenever they feel the need to escape.
- Pray for the person and the family and let them know that you are praying for them.
- Very importantly: Tell them you love them! Tell them a lot. They need to hear that they still matter to someone, and they need some measure of reassurance that they are not going to be abandoned further.
- Expressions of genuine kindness, tenderness, compassion, and empathy never fail to reach another person's heart.
- Allow them to keep talking about the person who has died. Don't make them feel they ever need to stop. Keep asking about them and keep telling your own stories and memories about them. They need to know that the person who is dead is not forgotten, that you miss them too, that they mattered, and that you still remember them.

Just think of things that the other grieving person might enjoy. Match up an idea that works and find the time to implement it. If it can't be accepted as planned don't give up, and try again. Remain flexible until you can spend quality time together.

Chapter 14

Time Is a Wound

I HAVE OFTEN HEARD people say that time heals every wound. Real grief is not healed by time. Time may even deepen our grief. Ulrike has been dead for many years. The perennial problem with death is absence. She has left a huge hole in the fabric of my life. There is no skirting around our suffering in grief. It will not dissolve on its own. If we are to incorporate this experience into our lives, we must walk through the center of our pain and learn to live with the grief we experience. Our culture often views grief as something almost entirely negative, as an aberration, a detour from a "normal" and happy life. However, if we understand that grief is an expression of love, we don't want to leave it behind. Instead, we learn to integrate it into our lives and to even appreciate it. This takes time. It is a lifelong process. As such it cannot be cheated, and it cannot be accelerated. We cannot fast-forward grief. When we feel driven to somehow get done with our grieving so that we may feel better sooner, we perhaps need to be reminded that in life many of the most profound experiences—like making love, eating, or drinking—are not necessarily better when they are done faster. Every living process, every story, requires time to shape and unfold. The relationship that has become so precious to me only grew with time. It should not surprise me, therefore, that the process of learning to live without her requires time too.

If a human being with whom we interact and are in contact still lives, this relationship has not come to an end. Our relationship can grow, it can mature, and we can shape and mold the relationship as it adapts to our decisions. But as soon as a living person dies, the relationship with this person cannot be changed anymore. Nothing in the relationship can be modified. Death brings something immutable, unalterable, and unchangeable. At death, everything is permanently fixed. It is final. The challenge is how to maintain a relationship with someone who was so significant and important in my life but who is no longer alive. Her life has come to an end, our living relationship has come to a standstill, and with it, there is an end to our active exchange of ideas, our communication, and our ability to participate in each other's lives. The finality of death, the finality of her absence, cannot be reversed. This emptiness is unchangeable, it is relentless and unyielding. Life cannot be brought back again. Here time becomes a double-edged sword. On the one hand, as time passed the sharp pain that I felt so acutely immediately after her death has eased. It has begun to lose its controlling power. It has receded more into the background. The edges of that emotional hole in my heart have grown less sharp. I can now better talk about it without being in perpetual danger of falling into the abyss of this void that is left through her absence. At the same time, however, with every passing day and every passing week the memory of her distinctive features gets weaker. Some of the characteristic qualities that made her who she was begin to fade in my mind. This scares me. It makes me sad. I want to remember her. I don't want to lose her. But who was she in her distinct individuality? It bothers me that I slowly forget the sound of her voice. I am ashamed to admit that I begin to forget the timbre of her laugh. I don't remember many details of our daily interactions that shaped my encounter with her. My porous memory leaks many of the details that made her who she was. Only some of her distinct features remain vivid in my memory. The ones I repeatedly share, I remember more distinctly, but I increasingly miss the full spectrum of her personality. This distresses and troubles me.

Time not only soothes the pain of loss it also creates new facets of separation. All the decisions that I make in time and space shape my character, determine who I am. They are instrumental in shaping my identity. But Ulrike is dead. She rests in the grave in an unconscious deep sleep (John 11:11–13; 1 Thess 4:13–18; Eccl 9:10). She knows nothing. She is dead. She is absent. She rests in peace. She does not know about any of our decisions. But we continue to live. We continue to develop and change. So how do we integrate her absence into our life?

Time Is a Wound
Integrating Death into Life

It requires courage and special skills to cope with loss and death. When we are in the space of grief and loss, we often wonder how to get back to a life of joy and happiness. I realized that this is impossible if we live in constant denial and if we are constantly bemoaning our situation. Healing is not realized in the absence of pain; it is rather the increased ability to meet our pain with mercy and grace.

Only by integrating the reality of death and grief into our lives can we learn to live a fulfilled life again. Only then can we take back our lives from what is sucking it away. As paradoxical as it may sound, accepting the death of the person you love so much and acknowledging your grief makes life more bearable. Learning to take back your life isn't a one-size-fits-all exercise. It is rather a unique, tailor-made task, where you figure out and decide in your daily challenges and joys what you need to do to regain and live your life to the fullest again.

In death a person ceases to exist physically. How can I integrate someone into my life who has ceased to exist, who is no longer present? How can I integrate the reality of Ulrike's death into my life if it is devoid of relationship? You can only integrate death in healing ways into your life if you don't deny the reality of death. The first step for integration is acknowledging this harsh reality. If I idealize the person as she was in the past, I would be stuck in a fake relationship in a lifeless past. I would be a prisoner of my own perceptions. I would be chained to my own imagination. I would continually be backward looking. I would stagnate in the past. I would not be free to grow. I know people who have never gotten over the death of their partner, or the death of their child. They tried to preserve and protect everything about this person in an idealized state of mind that is trapped in earlier times. They artificially preserve and maintain this lifeless past unchanged. Everybody around them quickly realizes that this does not work. Such an attitude is sick. It is not healthy and healing. I cannot preserve the past artificially in my thinking in a way that no longer matches present reality.

A concept that has helped me deal with my grief in healing ways has been what I would call hopeful remembrance. Hopeful remembrance is a memory that gratefully remembers what we experienced together, what united us in our shared joy, what influenced and shaped us and left an imprint on our character and lives, things that can be traced back to our common past. It is like the memory of a happy childhood.[1] A healthy person loves to think back to his or her happy upbringing. People love to remember and retell the positive things he or she experienced, and what we learned from the not so positive things in life. Yet, a healthy adult is not stuck in an infantile phase and will not act and behave like a little child! Our life—and time—has progressed. The circumstances we face have changed. We have changed. We have grown—not just physically, but mentally, spiritually, emotionally, and in our social competence. We have become more mature. Experiences and memories of the past help us to master the challenges of the present. In a similar way, the hopeful remembrance of the person who is no longer alive can inspire us in our decisions today. A hopeful remembrance is gratitude for the love and joy we shared. It is gratitude for all the small and big blessings we experienced together. It enables us to master the new reality of our lives with courage and in healing ways. Another exercise that has helped me discover gratitude and has enriched me and enabled me to flourish again and recover the beauty of life has to do with the art of learning to be grateful again.

Gratitude

The wound of parting through death always remains. That there could be a "bright side" to this enormous loss sounded so unreal, even offensive to me. Over time I began to understand that I am not a passive victim of a tragedy, rather I have the ability to influence and change the way I am thinking. When I surround my mind with thoughts of gratitude, I position myself for a significant change in my heart that improves the quality of my life. It changed my feelings. Some very practical, simple exercises to develop an attitude of gratitude have tremendously helped me change my perspective.[2] They have opened new horizons, enhanced the quality of my life, and improved my relationship with others. It helped me stay spiritually sane and even joyful.

Learning to be grateful again was key for me regaining my composure. When you experience significant loss such as the loss of your spouse, it is difficult to remember anything for which you want to be grateful. Ulrike

---

1. Even if someone had an unhappy childhood, I can remember my childhood and the things that formed me, and I can decide how to do things differently in the here and now.

2. You can read about it in Hasel, *Longing for God*, 68–69.

died in October. It was one of her favorite months. She loved the beautiful autumn colors when the leaves turned into magnificent orange, glowing red, bright yellow, and various shades of brown. The shimmering light of the autumn sun would fill the land with beautiful colors before the grey of winter would cover the land again. That first October after her death the brilliant autumn colors radiated in their beauty as they had done all the years before, but to me, everything appeared grey and not as colorful and beautiful anymore. I missed experiencing the autumn beauty together. Alone it was not the same.

The last thing I wanted to practice was gratitude. As a committed Christian, I knew that I should be grateful. But how do you develop an attitude of gratitude, if you don't feel thankful for what is happening in your life? How can you have an attitude of gratitude if you have the impression that there is nothing to be grateful for? Why should I be grateful at all, if life is unfair or does not treat me nicely? How can I be grateful if I don't get what I desire to have?

God knows how important gratitude is for our well-being. That is why he has invited his children to be persons who exercise gratitude and a spirit of thankfulness. "In everything give thanks; for this is the will of God in Christ Jesus for you," the apostle Paul writes in 1 Thess 5:18 (NASB). Thankfulness to God expresses our gratefulness for the very life he has given. That does not mean that everything in life is smooth or perfect. The world does not have to be perfect to be beautiful! Beauty greets and meets us in many places in nature, art, music, poetry, and the kindness of other people. It startles us in stunning ways and captures our attention. Like goodness, beauty is part of God's created reality. But it can be easily missed.[3] Developing an attitude of gratitude opens our eyes to the beautiful things in life or to particular people without demanding perfection all the time.[4] Interestingly, the word *gratitude* is derived from the Latin word *gratia*, which means "grace," "graciousness," or "gratefulness."

By practicing gratitude, we shift our attention from those imaginary things we don't have to the reality of the very things we (still) have. It grows out of an awareness of what we have been given. Such gratitude broadens our horizons. Instead of focusing on the things we lack we deliberately decide to reflect on the many things we still have and are still able to do.

---

3. On the startling presence of beauty in this world see the stimulating thoughts in Ganssle, *Our Deepest Desire*, 73–76.

4. See Fischer, *Heart*, 162.

Gratitude fosters a mindset that brings satisfaction in its wake. It raises awareness of the many opportunities and possibilities we have and how they can become a blessing—even for others, as we share what we have. It can be as simple as sharing a smile, a friendly gesture, a helping hand, or an embrace.

A Harvard Health publication has stated that gratitude is the healthiest emotion of all. "In positive psychology research, gratitude is strongly and consistently associated with greater happiness. Gratitude helps people feel more positive emotions, relish good experiences, improve their health, deal with adversity, and build strong relationships. Most studies published on this topic have found an association between gratitude and an individual's well-being."[5] Other research has confirmed these amazing findings. Dr. Martin E. P. Seligman, a leading researcher, and psychologist at the University of Pennsylvania, scientifically tested the impact of various positive psychological interventions on 411 people, each compared with a control assignment of writing about earlier memories. When they received the assignment to write and personally deliver a letter of gratitude to someone who had never been properly thanked for his or her kindness, participants immediately exhibited a huge increase in happiness scores. The study shows that the impact of this was greater than from any other intervention, and its positive effects lasted for a month.[6] No wonder God calls us to express our thankfulness. Imagine the tremendous well-being benefits you will receive: positive emotions, memories of good experiences, improved health, the ability to better cope with adverse situations and build stronger relationships as well as an increase in happiness, lasting up to a month, by simply exercising thankfulness and developing an attitude of gratitude. I know that this is not a silver bullet that will solve all our problems and it does not dissolve every difficulty and challenge we face. But my own story has taught me that gratitude opens a pathway to healing that would otherwise be crowded by my worries, fear, pain, and grief.

My aunt Hilde modeled such gratitude to me in a beautiful way. She could relate to my pain because her husband had died in a tragic car accident some years earlier. Despite the pain over her loss, she chose to remain grateful and challenged me to do the same. What I will share with you now sounds ridiculously simple but it has the power to change your life for the

---

5. Miller, "In Praise of Gratitude."

6. Seligman et al., "Empirical Validation of Interventions," 410–21, as quoted in Fischer, *Heart*, 163, 176.

better. Each day for one week, I wrote down on a sheet of paper ten words of things I was grateful for. Then I formed ten short sentences explaining why I was grateful for each thing. These sentences could even be turned into simple prayers. For example:

- *Eyes*. I am grateful for my eyes, because they allow me to see the colors and the faces of people I love.
- *Hands*. I am grateful for my hands, which allow me to write, play an instrument, do good, and touch other people.
- *Toothbrush*. I am grateful for my toothbrush because it helps my mouth to feel fresh and clean, which also helps give me confidence.

Once I had written down the short sentence, I voiced the sentence so that I could hear myself speaking those words. I repeated this exercise the next day with ten new things for which I was grateful. And if you want to intensify the practice, you may repeat the previous reasons for your gratefulness.

When I first started the practice, it was challenging to know what to write. Gratitude is like a muscle; the more you exercise it, the stronger it grows. At the end of just one week, I had seventy reasons to be grateful. But more than that, I gained a new perspective on life. Instead of focusing on what I didn't have, I increased my capacity to enjoy the "hidden" blessings that had been there all along. This exercise transformed my life for the better. It has only one disadvantage: it is completely free and does not cost a penny. If you can handle this drawback, you will realize its enormous blessing. So, I would like to challenge you, as I was challenged by my aunt, to write down ten things for which you are grateful for every day for the next week. After you have written down ten words (i.e., eyes, bed, friend, etc.) think for a moment about what these things actually mean to you (i.e., What do my eyes mean for me? What do they enable me to do that I would not be able to do if I were blind? What does my bed mean to me? How would my life change if I always had to sleep on a hard, cold floor? What does my friend mean to me? How would life be different if I didn't have this friend in my life?).

Then, take each word and write a short sentence, expressing your gratitude to God, the Giver of "every good gift and every perfect gift" (Jas 1:17). You can say, "Lord Jesus, thank you for my eyes with which I can see colors and read books. Thank you for my bed, that keeps me comfortable and warm. Thank you for my supportive friend that makes life so much more enjoyable. Thank you for . . ."

Next, speak each of these sentences out loud so that you can hear your voice. The more you engage your senses (seeing, touching, speaking, hearing) in expressing thankfulness, the more firmly the grateful thoughts will be fixed in your mind.

The next day, repeat the process with ten new things. If you want to intensify this experience, repeat the items from the previous day (or days). At the end of just one week, you will already have seventy reasons to be grateful! If you keep building the habit, gratitude will change your life for the better—guaranteed!

Learning to Love Again

Developing and cultivating an attitude of gratitude grew into an incredible blessing that enhanced my life and helped me to flourish again. Gratitude requires acute and attentive perception. In our grief fears and anxieties scream to make their presence known, sometimes in an overwhelming manner. But not so with gratitude. Gratitude is quieter and more gracious. It needs to be fostered and cultivated because it hides among the day to day and does not impose itself upon us. Only when I learned to cultivate gratitude did I develop a sensibility for life's perennial beauty. Still, there was so much more that I needed to learn and discover, to be able to love again and enjoy life. When my life is touched with kindness, in the middle of grief and pain, I realize, if ever so slightly, how the truth unfolds that love is meant to be.

In a recent meeting with young people, where I shared some of my experiences of significant loss, a young female participant asked whether I would marry my wife again if I knew how it would end. She wanted to know if it was worth the risk. After all many marriages will not end happily married forever. Reflecting on this question many years after I lost Ulrike, it did not take me long to answer. Yes, I would do it again! I would not want to miss what I enjoyed with her. To me, the experience of love is absolutely worth the risk. Why? Because true love does not calculate. True love IS. It is committed. True love experiences the beauty of love in unconditional commitment and faithfulness. I do not love another person because I know that we will have a life without any obstacles or that our lives would always have a happy ending. I loved Ulrike freely and unconditionally because I loved her. I would do it again. I love her. She loved me in the same way. I think experiencing a love that is not limited by other expectations or dependent on my performance is truly liberating and ennobling. It is like a glimpse of the divine. It is the foundation and essence of what it means to be human and to be created in the image of God. This is how God loves us. This is how love should be. Sometimes we think that the grief we experience is unbearable. In reality, the only unbearable thing that exists is the refusal to love in the first place. If we had no one we loved enough to mourn, how flat, how terribly boring our lives would be! When you think of this special person whom you love so much, and through whom you experienced such love, what would your life have been without them? Love is the reason why it is worth enduring the pain I am experiencing now without her. Hence, "grief dares us to love once more."[7]

Love is the salve and love is the cure. Love is the reason why new love and new relationships can grow even after the pain of death. Grieving can make a person harsh. It can harden the heart. Grieving can lead to isolation. The death of a loved one can make me ruminate and worry about the death of every other significant person in my life. Death confronts each of us with the reality of the biggest open secret: we all must die at some point. Even the people who are closest to us are not exempt from death just because we belong to each other. One way to react to this sobering realization and reality is to shut down our human impulses to connect and grow in relationships with others. That is why grieving often leads to inner isolation.

But love has the amazing ability to soften what has become hard as stone. Love fills new life into what feels like dead bones. Love is! Love is still there. Therefore, love is able to create something that did not exist before: community and fellowship. Love is the power that sustains us in our search for loving relationships. To lose someone in death and then continue to give love a chance, to experience the pain of loss and then continue to stay soft and open to the possibility of loving new people who are equally as mortal, to love someone and knowing full well the cost of our love, this is an act of bravery that often goes unnoticed. It is worthy of our recognition and admiration. I am always amazed at our capacity to love. To me, this is one of love's secrets. It is what makes us human because it entails an element of the divine that goes beyond what is humanly explainable. I believe God is the source and fountain of all love. All our human love is just a tiny little reel compared to the endless ocean of God's tender love for us. And so, through God's grace, out of the ashes of our pain comes the fire of new love

---

7. "living_through_loss," September 20, 2022.

and a hope that goes beyond this world. It echoes a spiritual reality that is sublimely divine and greater than our finite human existence.

Chapter 15

Epilogue

Two are rowing
One boat.
One is knowledgeable of the stars
The other is knowledgeable of the storms,
One will lead through the stars,
The other will lead through the storms,
And in the end, at the very end
The sea will be blue in our memory

Reiner Kunze[1]

THE STARS SHINE THE brightest when the night is the darkest. It is amazing that often in the darkest moments of our lives there are memories and people that shine like bright stars. Experiencing the death of a loved one is like a cold dark night. Looking at the stars, however, can change our perspective. The stars provide orientation and guide us on our journey. Without them, we are simply driven by the wind. With the stars, we can sail against the wind and reach our destination despite the headwind. On a cold and dark night, the stars are clearer, and we can see their beauty more distinctly. Even when the stars are covered by stormy clouds, we can remind ourselves that those dark clouds are saturated with mercy and that they will not exist forever. Eventually, the clouds will move and disappear,

---

1. Translation by Frank M. Hasel. The German original reads as follows: "*Rudern zwei ein boot, der eine kundig der sterne, der andre kundig der stürme, wird der eine führn durch die sterne, wird der andre führn durch die stürme, und am ende ganz am ende wird das meer in der erinnerung blau sein*" (Kunze, *Sensible Wege*, 9).

but the stars remain constant in their place. Their existence is not diminished by the clouds that temporarily cover them. Ancient navigators found their way through the endless waters of the mighty oceans by looking at the stars. They were not deterred by dark clouds. They knew they could rely on the unmovable stars of heaven. The experience of loss not only helps us to clarify what is really important to us, it also helps us to navigate the direction in which we want to continue our journey. For me, the guiding star of my life has been—and continues to be—the word of God. It testifies to God's amazing love for me. This love is higher than the stars and wider than the sky and deeper than the great waters. The word of God tells me of my origin and final destiny. It points to Jesus Christ my savior. It guides my life and provides valuable orientation. The ethical values it teaches make my life worth living. It also reminds me that "the Lord's lovingkindnesses indeed never cease, for His compassions never fail. They are new every morning. Great is Your faithfulness" (Lam 3:22–23 NASB). While death and grief can cause us to fall abysmally deep, we fall no deeper than into the loving arms of God. His arms are wide open to embrace and hold us fast and secure. His heart mourns with us and is touched by our grief. He is the one who sustains our life. He is the one who knows the stars and he is the one who masters the storms. And in the end, at the very end, the raging sea will be blue in our memory.

> Two are rowing
> one boat.
> There is a third One.
> HE knows the stars.
> HE masters the storms.
> HE will lead them through the stars.
> HE will lead them through the storms.
> And in the end, at the very end,
> the raging sea will be blue in our memory.
>
> Frank M. Hasel

Bibliography

Bates, Sasha. *Languages of Loss: A Psychotherapist's Journey through Grief.* London: Yellow Kite, 2020.
Bonhoeffer, Dietrich. *Letters and Papers from Prison.* Minneapolis: Fortress, 2010.
Buettner, Dan. "The Secrets of Long Life." *National Geographic* 208.5 (2005) 2–26.
Dallmann, William. *Paul Gerhardt: His Life and His Hymns.* St. Louis: Concordia, 1921.
Devine, Megan. *It's OK That You're Not OK: Meeting Grief and Loss in a Culture That Doesn't Understand.* Boulder: Sounds True, 2017.
Donnelly, Sue. "The Gate of the Year—Minnie Louise Haskins (1875–1957)." London School of Economics and Politics Science blog, December 10, 2013. https://blogs.lse.ac.uk/lsehistory/2013/12/10/the-gate-of-the-year-minnie-louise-haskins-1875-1957/.
Edelman, Hope. *The AfterGrief: Finding Your Way along the Long Arc of Loss.* New York: Ballantine, 2020.
Fischer, Suzanne Wood. *The Heart of the Amish: Life Lessons on Peacemaking and the Power of Forgiveness.* Grand Rapids: Revell, 2012.
Ganssle, Gregory E. *Our Deepest Desire: How the Christian Story Fulfills Human Aspirations.* Downers Grove, IL: InterVarsity, 2017.
Gerhardt, Paul. "Be Thou Content; Be Still Before." Translated by Catherine Winkworth. 1670. https://hymnary.org/text/be_thou_content_be_still_before.
———. "Commit Thou All That Grieves Thee." Translated by John Wesley. 1653. https://hymnary.org/text/commit_thou_all_thy_griefs.
Good News Network. "Quote of the Day." https://www.goodnewsnetwork.org/irish-saying-about-loss/.
Hasel, Frank M. *Living for God: Reclaiming the Joy of Christian Virtue.* Nampa, ID: Pacific, 2020.
———. *Longing for God: A Prayer and Bible Journal.* Nampa, ID: Pacific, 2017.
———. *Love Is! A Journey of Grief, Grace, and Gratitude.* Eugene, OR: Cascade, 2024.
Hickman, Martha Whitmore. *Healing after Loss: Daily Meditations for Working through Grief.* New York: William Morrow, 2002.
Kaléko, Mascha. *Verse für Zeitgenossen.* Reinbeck: Rowohlt, 2010.
Kübler-Ross, Elisabeth, and David Kessler. *On Grief and Grieving: Finding the Meaning of Grief through the Five Stages of Loss.* New York: Scribner, 2014.
Kunze, Reiner. *Sensible Wege und frühe Gedichte.* Frankfurt: Fischer Taschenbuch, 1995.
Lamott, Anne. *Bird by Bird: Some Instructions on Writing and Life.* New York: Anchor, 1995.

BIBLIOGRAPHY

Lewis, C. S. *A Grief Observed*. New York: HarperCollins, 1994.
living_through_loss. "All sorrows can be borne if you put them into a story or tell a story about them. —Isak Dinesen." Instagram post, September 9, 2021. https://www.instagram.com/p/CTmaiX5n88o/.
———. "Grief dares us to love once more. —Terry Williams." Instagram post, September 20, 2022. https://www.instagram.com/p/CivOhlcO8fi/.
McInerny, Nora. *The Hot Young Widows Club: Lessons on Survival from the Front Lines of Grief*. New York: Simon and Schuster, 2019.
Metaxas, Eric. *Bonhoeffer*. Nashville: Thomas Nelson, 2000.
Miller, Michael Craig. "In Praise of Gratitude." Harvard Health Blog, November 21, 2012. https://www.health.harvard.edu/blog/in-praise-of-gratitude-201211215561.
Nicola, Karen, and Steve Nicola. "Comfort for the Day: Grief Care and Education Resources." www.comfortfortheday.com.
Nolte, Andreas. *The Poems of Mascha Kaléko*. Burlington, VT: Fomite, 2017.
Peckham, John C. *Theodicy of Love: Cosmic Conflict and the Problem of Evil*. Grand Rapids: Baker Academic, 2018.
Rückert, Friedrich. *Die Weisheit des Brahmanen, ein Lehrgedicht in Bruchstücken*. Vol. 5. Leipzig: Bibliographisches Institut, 1897.
Sampson, Aubrey. *The Louder Song: Listening for Hope in the Midst of Lament*. Colorado Springs: NavPress, 2019.
Schubert, Helga. *Vom Aufstehen: Ein Leben in Geschichten*. Munich: dtv, 2021.
Schwartzberg, Louie. "Nature. Beauty. Gratitude." TED Talk, June 2011. https://www.ted.com/talks/louie_schwartzberg_nature_beauty_gratitude?language=en.
Seligman M. E. P., et al. "Empirical Validation of Interventions." *American Psychologist* 60.1 (2005) 410–21.
Shakespeare, William. "William Shakespeare Quotes." *AllGreatQuotes*. https://www.allgreatquotes.com/king-lear-quotes-395/.
Smith, Claire Bidwell. *Anxiety: The Missing Stage of Grief*. New York: Da Capo, 2018.
Stalin, Josef. "Josef Stalin Quotes." https://www.brainyquote.com/quotes/joseph_stalin_161352.
Tripp, Paul David. *Suffering: Gospel Hope When Life Doesn't Make Sense*. Wheaton: Crossway, 2018.
Vroegop, Mark. *Dark Clouds, Deep Mercy: Discovering the Grace of Lament*. Wheaton: Crossway, 2019.
Waltke, Bruce K., et al. *The Psalms as Christian Lament: A Historical Commentary*. Grand Rapids: Eerdmans, 2014.
Westermann, Claus. "The Role of Lament in the Theology of the Old Testament." *Interpretation: A Journal of Bible and Theology* 28.1 (1974) 20–38.
Wikipedia. "The Gate of the Year." https://en.wikipedia.org/wiki/The_Gate_of_the_Year#Text.
Wolterstorff, Nicholas. *Lament for a Son*. Grand Rapids: Eerdmans, 1987.

www.ingramcontent.com/pod-product-compliance
Lightning Source LLC
Chambersburg PA
CBHW032231080426
42735CB00008B/807